NORTHERN CALIFORNIA

History
Weekends

Fifty-two Adventures in History

BY LEE FOSTER

Sept. 2002
Larry + Dick —
Enjoy your weekend
away and here are
some ideas. for a few more
Love,
Dee + Brian

The Globe Pequot Press

Guilford, Connecticut

About the Author

Lee Foster is an award-winning travel writer/photographer living in Berkeley, California. Raised in Minnesota, educated at Stanford, Lee has resided in Northern California for most of his adult life. As a travel journalist, Lee has covered more than 200 worldwide destinations. He has won numerous travel journalism awards, including six Lowell Thomas Awards. History and nature are two of his favorite travel subjects. You can see more of his work on the Web at www.fostertravel.com.

Cover design by Libby Kingsbury
Text design by Lisa Reneson
Maps by M.A. Dube
Cover photo of the Golden Gate Bridge by Ewing Galloway/Index Stock
All other photographs by the author

Library of Congress Cataloging-in-Publication Data
Foster, Lee, 1943–
   Northern California history weekends: fifty-two adventures in history/Lee Foster.—1st ed.
     p. cm.
   Includes index.
   ISBN 0-7627-1076-4
   1. California, Northern—Guidebooks. 2. Historic sites—California, Northern—Guidebooks. 3. California, Northern—History, Local. I. Title.

F867.5 .F67 2001
917.9404'54—dc21   2001040574

Manufactured in the United States of America
First Edition/First Printing

This book is dedicated to
Bart, Karin, and Paul
—my future in California.

Acknowledgments

A number of my friends and colleagues in Northern California tourism were good enough to review individual chapters and offer comments. Thanks to:

Hank Armstrong, Julie Armstrong, Laurie Armstrong, Susan Arthur, Jan Austerman, Glen Boire, Amy Breall, Ellen Briggs, Kelli Coane, Cammie Conlon, Gay Eitel, Kris Fister, Miriam Guiney, Greg Hayes, Barbara Hillman, Amanda Holder, Susan Julian, Malei Jessee, Ellen Kohler, Him Mark Lai, Jan Leroy, Carol McCall, Sue Mauro, Charise McHugh, J. D. O'Rourke, Claudia Pehar, John Poimiroo, Sharon Rooney, Fred Sater, Bonnie Sharp, Hal Schell, Karen Schmauss, Tony Smithers, Lucy Steffens, Cathy Stevenson, Lora Vance, Bill Walton, and Phil Weidinger.

Help Us Keep This Guide Up to Date

Every effort has been made by the author and editors to make this guide as accurate and useful as possible. However, many things can change after a guide is published—establishments close, phone numbers change, facilities come under new management, etc.

We would love to hear from you concerning your experiences with this guide and how you feel it could be improved and kept up to date. While we may not be able to respond to all comments and suggestions, we'll take them to heart and we'll also make certain to share them with the author. Please send your comments and suggestions to the following address:

The Globe Pequot Press
Reader Response/Editorial Department
P.O. Box 480
Guilford, CT 06437

Or you may e-mail us at:

editorial@globe-pequot.com

Thanks for your input, and happy travels!

Contents

Napa and Sonoma

Redwood Country

Shasta-Cascade Region

Sacramento and the Gold Country

The Sierra

Monterey–Big Sur and Santa Cruz

Introduction

From the accidental discovery of gold to the ongoing drama of saving the mighty redwoods, Northern California possesses the richest historical story in the West. Even the name "California" has storied beginnings: it was coined by Spanish novelist Garci Ordonez de Montalvo, who imagined a terrestrial paradise populated by Amazon beauties.

For the first inhabitants of Northern California—especially the Ohlone Indians around San Francisco Bay—life was comfortable, with ample fish, shellfish, game, acorns, and seeds. The first European settlement in Northern California, the Presidio, was established at San Francisco as a Spanish fort by Juan Bautista de Anza in 1776. The Gold Rush of 1848 transformed the face of San Francisco and Northern California. Within a few years the pastoral scattering of Spanish-Mexican dwellings with a modest population became a restless prospecting region of 250,000. Statehood came in 1850, and by 1852 an estimated $200 million in gold had been mined in the foothills and shipped to the treasure houses of San Francisco.

The true "mother lode," however, proved to exist not in the rock scrabble of mountain streams but in the vast, fertile farmlands of the Central Valley and the cooler fruit-growing coastal valleys. Agriculture, not gold mining, was the path to assured wealth.

The Great Earthquake shook San Francisco on April 18, 1906, but the Great Fire that followed actually caused more damage. Fed by broken natural gas lines and unchecked because the city's water mains had been destroyed by the quake, the fire raged for three days, consuming 28,000 buildings. Those circa 1860 to 1900 Victorian houses that survived have become as much a symbol of the city as the cable cars or the Golden Gate Bridge.

In the modern era Northern California has prospered because of Silicon Valley inventiveness. And while many other regions of the country have allowed uncontrolled growth to trash their environments, Northern California has established numerous safeguards. These public decisions range from preserving much of the coast to saving substantial redwood forests.

There is simply so much engaging California history to explore. And it can all be found within a weekend trip from San Francisco. Every decade of the state's history produced lasting effects, for both the United States and the World. To understand how the transcontinental railroad united the country and created a huge national market, visit Old Sacramento's excellent Railroad

The Winchester Mystery House in San Jose features architectural oddities such as doors opening into walls and stairs going nowhere.

Museum. To appreciate the environmental movement in California, take a trip to the famous campout site in Yosemite where conservationist John Muir hosted then president Theodore Roosevelt. To learn more about the Silicon Valley innovations that have changed the way the world communicates, stop in at the Tech Museum in San Jose.

Whether you have an hour, a day, or an entire weekend, Northern California is ideal for a historic getaway. The diverse landscape is lush and inviting. The weather is temperate, allowing for an engaging trip every weekend of the year, and the travel amenities offered here—cozy inns, world-class wines, and choice dining—are among the finest you'll find anywhere.

How to Use This Book

This book is laid out in the logical manner that would suit an explorer of Northern California history. Begin with discoveries in San Francisco and the immediate Bay Area, from the Alcatraz prison island to Leland Stanford's famous "farm" in Palo Alto, now Stanford University.

Look north for short day and overnight trips to learn more about Sir Francis Drake's landing at Point Reyes or writer Robert Louis Stevenson's stay in the Napa Wine Country. Once your taste for historic exploration beckons, an overnight/two-night trip to Redwood Country or the Lake Shasta area can be tempting.

Looking east, a day trip to Old Sacramento—where the Gold Rush miners set out from—can get you started. Then an overnight/weekend trip to the Gold Country or the glories of Lake Tahoe and Yosemite might follow.

Toward the south, the historic Beach Boardwalk in Santa Cruz, or the first park where redwoods were set aside (Big Basin) can be explored on a day trip. Then the collection of historic adobes along Monterey's Path of History or writer John Steinbeck's legacy in Salinas may intrigue you for an overnight trip.

Most of these historic journeys can be enjoyed at any time of the year, but there are sometimes festivals or natural seasonal phenomena that make certain times even more special. The Mendocino Whale Festival occurs in March when the gray whales migrate from Baja, Mexico, north to their summer home in Alaska. Each May Fireman's Muster at Columbia re-creates the world of the fire brigades in the wood-constructed towns of the Gold-Rush era. Salinas celebrates author John Steinbeck's legacy at an annual festival in August. For ideas on trips for specific months, see Festivals in Northern California on page 4.

Planning Your Trip

Each of the fifty-two sections in this book is laid out in a consistent pattern designed to make your trip enjoyable and informative.

The historic story details the historic significance of what you will see.

Getting there includes practical details about which roads to take and where to go.

Be sure to see lists the main features not to miss during your visit.

Best time to visit alerts you to any seasonal factors that might have a bearing on the trip.

Lodging offers a good lodging option in the area, often in an establishment with special historic significance.

Dining presents a quality dining experience, also chosen for its historic value where appropriate.

For more information provides contact information on local tourism offices. In this Internet era, the Web sites of tourism entities and travel providers offer excellent supplementary information for planning your trip.

With all this in mind, your author wishes you many joyous weekends exploring the historic treasures of Northern California.

Festivals in Northern California

Many of the weekend outings described in this book can be enjoyed any time of the year. However, some coincide with special festivities that you might want to consider. Here is a guide to outings with a festival in mind.

June

July

August

September

October

December

101

80

4

24

1

Angel Island
State Park

Alcatraz
Island

6 • Berkeley

680

5

Golden Gate

80

7 • Oakland

580

1

San
Francisco

2 3 4

280

280

101

San
Francisco
Bay

92

880

Pacifica • 35

280

Montara •
Point Montara
Lighthouse

San Mateo •

Belmont •

92

San Carlos • 12

84

101

84

Stanford
University

11 •

680

Woodside •

13

see San Mateo
Peninsula map
on page 62

84

35

280

Santa Clara
•

8 10

680

9

San Jose •

1

• Pescadero

35

Pacific
Ocean

17

Driving Tour

0   5   10

MILES

Pigeon
Point
Lighthouse

17

San Francisco Bay Area

1

San Francisco Bay Area

The Golden Gate Bridge: Spanning the Gap

Whether viewed from its south- or north-end viewpoints or from the deck of an excursion boat, the Golden Gate Bridge is an amazing sight—a glorious creation born of political vision and technical imagination.

The historic story

Emperor Norton, a San Francisco character of the 1860s, is credited with the first public proposals for a bridge, and railroad magnate Charles Crocker presented actual plans in the 1870s. The task was enormous, and public interest dwindled until 1916, when newspaperman James Wilkins launched an editorial campaign favoring a bridge. The idea especially appealed to North Bay residents, who were transporting their cars on time-consuming ferries. Spanning the Golden Gate, however, seemed more like a dream than a possibility. In 1917 San Francisco's chief engineer, M. M. O'Shaughnessy, enlisted the aid of Chicago engineer Joseph B. Strauss to design and build the bridge.

A distinguished bridge builder, Strauss engineered over 400 bridges from Leningrad to New Jersey in his lifelong record. He followed the Golden Gate project attentively for the next two decades, and a statue at the south end of the bridge acknowledges his role as "The Man Who Built The Bridge."

But first, the political hurdles had to be surmounted. In 1930 voters in the six counties making up the Bridge District approved the bonds to finance it. This act required some vision as the nation waded through the Depression. In January 1933 Strauss broke ground for construction of the towers. Admirably, the bridge was completed on time and under its $35 million budget, with the last bridge bond paid off in 1971. Today's toll goes entirely to main-

The Golden Gate Bridge was the longest suspension bridge of its time.

taining the bridge, including its never-ending painting schedule.

One main technical challenge in the 1930s construction involved the 4,200-foot length of the span, which many said could not be bridged successfully. Strauss weighed plans for a suspension bridge, which risked being too flimsy, and a cantilever bridge, which seemed too heavy for the site. At the time, a suspension bridge of this length hadn't been attempted, and Strauss's original design incorporated both ideas. From an aesthetic point of view, his later decision to focus on the suspension approach proved far superior.

The location of the bridge, bearing the full brunt of the ocean elements, exacerbated potential design problems. Winds of 20 to 60 miles per hour are commonplace, and a broadside wind of 100 miles per hour produces a midspan sway of 21 feet, which had to be allowed for. Heat and cold–caused expansion and contraction would raise and lower the bridge by 10 feet. The depth of the water underneath the bridge and the speed of the current also presented major technical challenges. Pacific tidal pressures are enormous in the narrow outlet, especially when the 7½-knot tidal outrush combines with the swift-flowing waters of the Sacramento and San Joaquin Rivers emptying through this gap into the ocean. Strauss decided to anchor one of the sixty-five-story towers right in the waterway, 1,215 feet from shore.

The 36½-inch cables manufactured for the bridge were the largest bridge cables ever made, incorporating 80,000 miles of wire about the thickness of a pencil. Each of the two cables had a tensile strength of 200 million pounds. During construction Strauss paid particular attention to worker safety. It was assumed in bridge building that one worker would die for every million dollars' worth of construction, but the safety record on the Golden Gate Bridge was excellent until near the end of the project.

A falling beam crushed an iron worker in 1936, and another tragic incident in February 1937 took ten lives when a scaffolding collapsed. A special net had saved nineteen men who fell at various times during construction, but the weight of the scaffolding tore through the safety net, carrying the workers to their death below.

Over the years the bridge has set some remarkable and gruesome records. Over 100,000 cars a day cross it between San Francisco and Marin County and the Redwood Country to the north. By February 1986 the billionth car had driven across. More than 1,200 people have jumped to their death from the span; to reduce sensational publicity and preclude copycat actions, the precise figure is no longer given out to the media.

Getting there

The Golden Gate Bridge is at the northernmost tip of San Francisco, accessible by car or taxi. Take the Highway 101 approach to the bridge and turn off at the last northbound San Francisco exit, which is clearly marked. The exit will take you to the observation area.

Be sure to see

Park your car at the south end of the Golden Gate Bridge. Spend some time enjoying the landscape and waterscape unfolding before you. The gracefulness of the bridge's suspension construction, its pleasing proportions alongside the green hills of Marin County to the north, and its orange-vermilion color against the blue sky and sea add to the picturesque effect. The ship lane below the Golden Gate Bridge has become its own bridge to the Orient, adding to the mystique of the site. Walk or bicycle onto the bridge and enjoy the cityscape of San Francisco, the fresh air, and the sense of grandeur the bridge inspires. A walk on the Golden Gate Bridge can be as memorable in California as your first view of Yosemite's El Capitan. A vista turnout at the north end of the bridge provides an inspiring view of the San Francisco skyline.

The Restoration of Crissy Field

Tucked between the Golden Gate Bridge and the Marina Green along the San Francisco waterfront is a major new amenity—restored Crissy Field—dedicated in June 2001.

Originally Crissy Field was a tidal marsh and a sandy, windswept landscape along the water. The tidal marsh was filled in for the 1915 Panama Pacific International Exposition and the sandy strip was transformed into a U.S. Army Airfield in 1921 to guard the Golden Gate.

As military air needs developed, the small size of the field made it obsolete. For a long time Crissy Field was known primarily as a polluted and junked up area covered over in asphalt.

In the 1990s Crissy Field went through a rebirth and by the June 2001 dedication, the tidal marsh had been restored, native vegetation planted, and a 28-acre sodded meadow opened for picnics and kite flying. Walking, jogging, in-line skating, and biking paths now link the Marina Green and Golden Gate Bridge through Crissy Field. Signage along the walk recalls the bi-plane heyday of the 1920s. Historic Crissy Field now offers one of the most agreeable fresh-air rambles available in any American city.

Best time to visit

Except for periods of summer fog, which can obscure the bridge for days, there is no bad season for viewing the Golden Gate Bridge. Somber fog or ingratiating sunlight both suit the structure and may fit the varying moods of the observer. Spring and autumn present the classic blue-sky days that avid bridge-watchers savor.

Lodging

Entrepreneur Bill Kimpton spent decades rescuing derelict San Francisco buildings and restoring them to first-class boutique hotels. Hotel Monaco (501 Geary Street, San Francisco, CA 94102; 415–292–0100; www.monaco-sf.com) is a fine example of his achievements.

Dining

Alioto's (8 Fisherman's Wharf; 415–673–0183) gets the nod as the romantic, fine-dining choice on Fisherman's Wharf. Nunzio Alioto, a Sicilian immigrant, first opened a fish stall here in 1925. Smooth career waiters bring out a platter of the various fresh fish available for the day.

For more information

The overall San Francisco information source for travelers is the San Francisco Convention and Visitors Bureau, 201 Third Street, Suite 900, San Francisco, CA 94103; 415–391–2000; www.sfvisitor.org. To receive their free Visitor Guide, write the Bureau at P.O. Box 429097, San Francisco, CA 94142-9097.

2

San Francisco Bay Area

San Francisco Cable Cars: Visiting the Cable Car Barn

No other American city evokes such images of romance—sweeping hills studded with pastel Victorians, the clanking of cable cars, the wail of foghorns, the glow of the Golden Gate Bridge at sunset. And where else can you ride around on a National Historic Landmark?

The historic story

The charming cable cars, perhaps the most endearing mode of transport in America, are a wonderful way to see much of San Francisco. Originally the impulse to build the cable car system came from the sickening but familiar sight of horses slipping on the steep hills in wet weather and breaking their legs. The birth of the cable car notion began in the 1870s with the offended sensibility of a manufacturer of iron cable, Andrew Smith Hallidie. While climbing the steep Jackson Street hill, he saw a horse-drawn car loaded with passengers proceed slowly up the hill, then falter as the lead horse lost its footing. The car slid quickly downhill, fortunately without loss of human life. However, the fallen lead horse pulled down the other horses, which suffered broken legs and mutilated muscles and had to be shot.

Hallidie went home shaking his head, thinking there must be a better way. Working alone and at his own expense, Hallidie devised a cable car system, finally putting it into operation on August 2, 1873. Hallidie took the first ride downhill alone; no one would ride with him. The San Franciscans in attendance were as skeptical as the modern traveler, who wonders what would happen if the car broke loose. When Hallidie proved the safety of the

Cable Car Routes

San Francisco's historic cable cars offer a one-of-a-kind touring experience.

concept, the popularity of cable cars soared.

The cable cars were completely restored in the 1980s and the line newly opened. Cars on the three branches of the line are now painted in the original nineteenth-century colors, such as maroon with cream and blue trim. There were eight active cable car companies in the 1890s, covering the city with 127 miles of track at the peak of cable car transport. Today there is one combined line with 10.5 miles of track in three branches.

Board at any place along the routes: Powell to Fisherman's Wharf, Powell to Hyde, and California from Market to Van Ness. Waiting lines to ride the cable cars are sometimes long, unfortunately, especially at Powell and Market. Drivers will collect fares after you have boarded.

Leave some time in your schedule for a visit to the Cable Car Barn and Museum (1201 Mason Street at Washington; 415–474–1887), where you can view the historic record and see the timeless paraphernalia that is the inner workings of the system. At the barn you can watch the huge wheels that pull the cable cars slowly to the stars.

When you enter the Cable Car Museum, you can visit the observation gallery or descend into the sheave (pronounced *shiv*) room to view the system's underground operation. Sheaves are the pulleys used in the system.

Large 750-horsepower engines turn a massive steel wheel, which pulls the thick cable, capable of hauling thirty-one six-ton cars up a 21 percent grade at a speed of 9.5 miles per hour.

One of the treasures of the museum is an original car from Andrew Hallidie's Clay Street Hill Railroad. This grip car, #8, dates from the 1870s.

Getting there

Cable Cars thread their way through the heart of San Francisco. The most typical boarding spot is at the foot of Powell, but you can board anywhere along the three routes.

Be sure to see

The three cable car lines offer an excellent open-air way to view the various parts of the central city, from Union Square nearly to Fisherman's Wharf, from the Embarcadero to Nob Hill. The Cable Car Museum will acquaint you with the inner workings of the system.

Best time to visit

The cable cars run all year. Each July there is a Cable Car Bell Ringing Contest, an entertaining event. The various cable car operators compete with their nuanced rings. The event is an only-in-San Francisco affair. Call the Cable Car Museum for the exact date and location.

Lodging

The Huntington, on the cable car route, sits on Nob Hill, residential area for the richest people of the city before the Quake of 1906 shook or burned down most of their palaces. The word "nob" is a shortened form of the term "nabob," a nineteenth-century expression for people of wealth and prominence. The Huntington's Big Four restaurant recalls the moguls who built the Central Pacific Railroad. A quiet, dignified, and exclusive lodging, the Huntington Hotel is at 1075 California Street, San Francisco, CA 94108; (800) 227–4683; www.huntingtonhotel.com.

Dining

Fior d'Italia in North Beach (601 Union Street at Stockton; 415–986–1886) has been in operation for more than 114 years and claims to be "America's oldest Italian restaurant." Try the Northern Italian creations.

For more information

The overall San Francisco information source for travelers is the San Francisco Convention and Visitors Bureau, 201 Third Street, Suite 900, San Francisco, CA 94103; 415–391–2000; www.sfvisitor.org. To receive a free Visitor Guide, write the Bureau at P.O. Box 429097, San Francisco, CA 94142-9097.

3

San Francisco Bay Area

Historic Chinatown: The Cantonese Enclave

Want to visit the Orient in a single weekend? Just walk through the dragon-crested portals of San Francisco's Chinatown and explore the hustle and bustle of another world.

The historic story

Chinese nationals were among the many people who sought their fortunes in the California Gold Rush. In the 1860s thousands of Chinese workers also came to construct the Central Pacific Railroad.

In the 1880s Scots writer Robert Louis Stevenson mused away his time here, just as hundreds of San Franciscans still do every day, and it was at Portsmouth Square that the first U.S. flag was raised in San Francisco, in 1846. Today a stone bridge links Portsmouth Square with the Chinese Culture Center (750 Kearny Street; 415–986–1822), third floor of the Holiday Inn hotel building. The Center sponsors interpretive exhibits about Chinese life in America and organizes guided walks through the area. Tai chi chuan practitioners exercise in the early morning at Portsmouth Square. Later in the day children and older adults enjoy the sun of the park, the pigeons, and Chinese chess.

Other historical displays can be seen at the Chinese Historical Society of America Museum, 644 Broadway, Fourth Floor; (415) 391–1188. The museum reminds a traveler that 80 percent of the Chinese in the United States trace their roots to a small region in Guangdong Province about the size of the San Francisco Bay Area. In the nineteenth century overpopulation and wars caused many farm families to urge their sons to emigrate.

A temple on Waverly is open to visitors and instructs on the spirituality

The architectural details of Chinatown's buildings reflect Asian influences.

of the Chinese. Visit the Tin How Temple (125 Waverly Street) to see the offerings of oranges, rice, and tea to ancestors and to the gods. Incense burns constantly in this restful and meditative setting of carved buddhas and red lanterns. The building housing the temple exhibits a colorful facade, as do the other temples, such as the Norras Temple, on this quiet street running parallel to Grant.

The opening of trade with mainland China in the 1970s gave Chinatown another renewal. In the past decade Chinatown has been rejuvenated by thousands of immigrants from Hong Kong, filling the gap created when Chinese moved to other locations in the community, such as the prosperous Richmond District, now a Chinese stronghold.

Chinatown, sometimes dubbed Cathay-by-the-Bay, is an ethnic capital for the 1.6 million Americans who are of Chinese descent.

Getting there

Chinatown comprises 24 blocks in the heart of San Francisco. Enter through the gates where Grant Avenue intersects Bush Street.

Be sure to see

Beyond the gates at Grant and Bush, stroll the area bounded by Stockton, Broadway, Kearny, and Bush.

Stockton between Washington and Broadway is where you'll find the largest concentration of markets, exhibiting an amazing array of vegetables and meats. Food markets stock vegetables such as Chinese bok choy and live meat, including pigeons. Numerous fat ducks hang raw or cooked, and baskets of paper-thin dried fish are on display. On Stockton you may even see a butcher carve up a pig or crates of chickens.

Jade and ivory carving can be seen at many shops, such as Jade Empire (832 Grant Street). The oldest grocery here is Mow Lee (774 Commercial Street), dating from 1856.

The Man Fung China Trading Company (638 Broadway) stocks a spectrum of People's Republic materials, ranging from dried mushrooms to down jackets, lacquerware to landscapes hand-painted on eggshells. The New China Book Store (642 Pacific) carries extensive literature portraying visions of life and thought in the People's Republic.

In St. Mary's Square there is a Benjamin Bufano sculpture of Dr. Sun Yat-sen, founder of the Chinese Republic (1911–1913).

If you're in San Francisco for the February celebration of Chinese New Year, you'll witness an urban cacophony of unparalleled dimension. The Chinese, who are said to have invented fireworks, know how to raise the decibel level in the urban canyons as the traditional Chinese Dragon snakes its way along the parade route to begin a new lunar calendar year. This second-largest Chinese enclave outside Asia (New York's Chinatown is larger) presents a spectrum of activities over a weeklong celebration, but the night of the big parade offers the best public access to the phenomenon.

Chinatown is a city within a city, a truly fascinating and foreign place.

Best time to visit

Any time of the year is good for Chinatown, but the Chinese New Year in February is special. Part of the fascination of occidentals with the Chinese New Year festivities is the lunar calendar. The Chinese rotate the years sequentially among twelve different creatures. This year's animal will be replaced in future annual changings of the animal guard by the ram, monkey, rooster, dog, boar, rat, ox, tiger, hare, dragon, serpent, and horse. The personality characteristics of the ruling animal deity in this Chinese zodiac are said to govern the year.

A visitor during the Chinese New Year period is likely to be greeted with the phrase "gung hay fat choy" or "may you prosper."

Lodging

In keeping with the weekend's theme, stay at the Mandarin Oriental (222 Sansome Street, San Francisco, CA 94104; 415–276–9888; www. mandarinoriental.com). This elegant financial-district location is known for its impeccable service.

Dining

Henry's Hunan Restaurant (110 Natoma Street; 415–546–4999) is a critically acclaimed Chinese restaurant. Innovative preparations breathe vitality into familiar-sounding dishes. Try the Henry's Special (chicken, shrimp, and scallops), named for chef-founder Henry Chung.

For more information

The overall San Francisco information source for travelers is the San Francisco Convention and Visitors Bureau, 201 Third Street, Suite 900, San Francisco, CA 94103; (415) 391–2000; www.sfvisitor.org. To receive their free Visitor Guide, write the Bureau at P.O. Box 429097, San Francisco, CA 94142-9097.

4

San Francisco Bay Area

San Francisco Victorians: The Legacy Spared

Although 28,000 buildings were destroyed in the Great Earthquake and Fire of 1906, impressive pockets of Victorian architecture survived—beautiful reminders of the elegance of days gone by. Spend a pleasant outing driving and walking past these historic homes, then enjoy a picnic lunch in Alamo Square.

The historic story

There were three main Victorian design styles—Italianate, Queen Anne, and Stick-Eastlake. Italianate, in vogue 1850–1870, has bay windows whose side windows slant inward, pipe-stem columns flanking the front door, and flat crowns over the doors and windows. Queen Anne, patterned after a style popular in England in the 1860s, is marked by rounded corners, hooded domes, and the use of shingles for siding. Stick-Eastlake is similar to Italianate but from a later period, mainly the 1880s, and is noted for chamfered corners on pillars, incised decoration, and horseshoe arches.

To view the best of the Victorians follow these directions. (Directions are precise, due to the one-way streets.) Start at Franklin and California. From the right, westbound lane on California, turn right on Franklin, left on Pacific, left on Scott, left on Clay, right on Steiner, right on Sacramento, left on Divisadero, left on Golden Gate, right on Scott skirting Alamo Square via Hayes and Steiner, left on McAllister, right on Divisadero, right on Bush, and left on Laguna to Union (see map on opposite page).

The word "Victorian" honors the memory of Britain's Queen Victoria, recalling popular architecture from her reign (1837–1901). Many Victorians

Victorian Driving Route

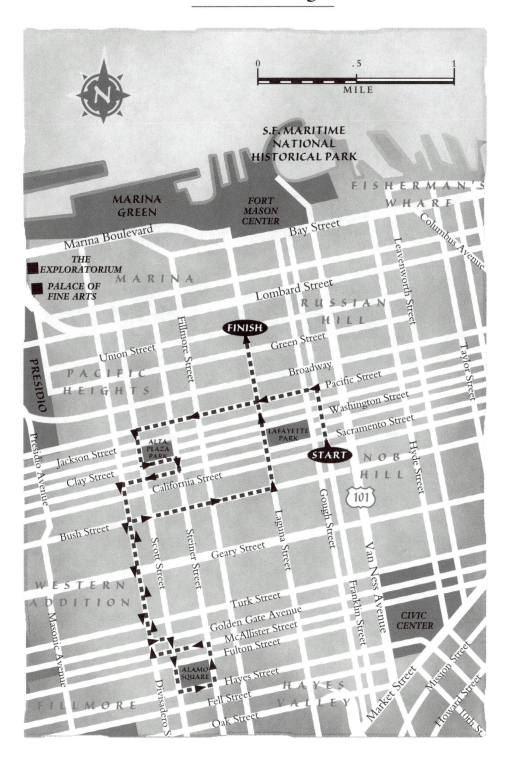

The stately Victorians as viewed from Alamo Square compete with the modern architecture of downtown.

were designed as prefabs and shipped around the Horn from New England after being ordered from catalogs. The people who buy and restore Victorians often have a passion for historic accuracy. Fairly audacious paint decoration, for example, was an important part of adornment in the Victorian era. Some owners have gone to great pains to re-create specific paint hues of the era.

Getting there

Start in San Francisco at the corner of Franklin and California.

Be sure to see

You'll want to linger at the miniparks, such as Alamo Square, for a break during this drive. But your main question might be: What Victorian could I see from the inside?

You can tour the lovely Haas-Lilienthal House, 2007 Franklin Street, built in 1886. This exuberant and classic Queen Anne building, designed by architect Peter Schmidt, has gables, bay windows, and turret towers. The interior boasts much of its original furniture and artifacts, with mahogany walls, marble hearths, and fine tapestries. The family lived in this house until 1972, leaving a display of family photos in the downstairs supper room. Call (415) 441–3004 to make reservations to view the house interior. The same number takes reservations for a two-hour Sunday walking tour of area Victorians that leaves from in front of the house. The organization behind all this nurturing of historic architecture is San Francisco Heritage; www.sfheritage.com.

Other prominent Victorians not to miss an outside look at are the Spreckels Mansion, 2080 Washington, and 2090 Jackson Street. Streets adjacent to Lafayette Square offer many other examples of Victorians.

At 1000 California Street stands the James Flood Mansion, built in 1886 by the Comstock Lode silver millionaire. Today the Flood Mansion on Nob Hill is the last of the great mansions from the baronial days of the mining and railroad kings. Now it serves as the home of the Pacific Union Club. Other mansions in the neighborhood were swept away in the fires that followed the Quake. Only 14,000 structures survived, mainly west of Van Ness Avenue.

Nob Hill must have had a remarkable appearance in that great period before the Quake and Fire of 1906. On Nob Hill were the grand houses of the "Big Four" directors of the Central Pacific Railroad—Leland Stanford, Mark Hopkins, Charles Crocker, and Collis P. Huntington. To this select group of structures were added the palaces of the "Silver Kings" of Nevada's Comstock Lode, James G. Fair and James C. Flood.

The Victorian era also included some fads and fashions in house building. One such passion was the construction of eight-sided or "octagon" houses. Today you can still see some octagon houses that escaped the Quake and Fire. One good example is the Feusier Octagon House at 1067 Green Street, built in 1855. Another octagon is at 2648 Gough Street.

Best time to visit

Any time of the year is good for Victorian viewing.

Lodging

The Archbishop's Mansion (1000 Fulton Street, San Francisco, CA 94117; 415–563–7872; www.arbishopsmansion.com) is now a B&B. Each room creates an atmosphere reminiscent of a nineteenth-century opera. The property is a handsome Victorian in the Alamo Square area, surrounded by other notable survivors of the 1906 Quake.

Dining

One of the most distinguished—and definitely the oldest—San Francisco restaurant is Tadich Grill (240 California Street; 415–391–2373). Tadich is known for its grilled seafood and career waiters. Some of the diners will tell you how their grandfathers once ate here. Tadich has been serving food since 1849 and claims to be one of the first one hundred businesses in California.

For more information

Contact the San Francisco Convention and Visitors Bureau, 201 Third Street, Suite 900, San Francisco, CA 94103-3152; (415) 391–2000; www.sfvisitor. com. To receive their free Visitor Guide, write the Bureau at P.O. Box 429097, San Francisco, CA 94142-9097.

5

San Francisco Bay Area

Alcatraz and Angel Islands: The Prison and Hope

In the middle of San Francisco Bay, occupying some of the choicest real estate on the planet, are two historic islands that symbolize widely different concepts—Alcatraz Island for despair and Angel Island State Park for hope. Take a ferry into the past and enjoy the stunning views both on the islands and along the way.

The historic story

While Alcatraz Penitentiary was designed during the height of the gangster era as the safest possible place to lock up the likes of Al Capone, Angel Island served as the Ellis Island of the West for immigrants from the Orient, who waited anxiously for their fate to be determined. Would they be allowed entry to the United States or be sent back to China? Angel Island was also a military fortification for more wars that one might imagine—the Civil War, Spanish American War, World War I, World War II, and the Cold War. Alcatraz was selected as a federal penitentiary (1934–1963) so that there would be no possibility of escape. Alcatraz became synonymous with maximum security, a symbol of American resolve at the time when mobsters seemed more powerful than law enforcement officers. Today about 1.2 million visitors a year journey to the island prison voluntarily.

Al "Scarface" Capone, George "Machine Gun" Kelly, and Robert "Birdman" Stroud were among the 1,576 involuntary residents who served time on Alcatraz. Thirty-six convicts were involved in fourteen escape attempts; five inmates disappeared in San Francisco Bay; and two who made the 1.25 miles to land were recaptured. No successful escapes have been confirmed.

Alcatraz Island was chosen as a prison site because escape through the chilly bay waters was unlikely.

So popular are the National Park Service tours of the island that reservations are highly recommended (415–773–1188).

Once on the island, you can tour the main cell block of the prison on your own with an audiocassette on which former inmates and guards act as tour guides. Ranger-led tours are also available. There is a hiking trail, the Agave Trail, around the southern shore. This steep trail has 110 steps and is open only in months when protected birds are not nesting.

The use of Alcatraz as a prison for civilians was only its most recent role. Starting in 1854, Alcatraz was a lighthouse. Fortified in 1859, there were one hundred cannons and 300 soldiers on Alcatraz at the time of the Civil War. Gradually, formidable Alcatraz began to take on the role of military prison, preparing itself for its federal civilian prison role.

Angel Island's story is more complex and joyful than that of Alcatraz. Ferries from San Francisco and Tiburon can take you to the island, where you can explore on foot or on bicycle.

Angel Island's history falls into several episodes—the Indian story, the

Spanish discovery, the use of the island as a military outpost and quarantine center, and the final role of the island as an immigrant waystop.

Miwok Indians used the island as a hunting and fishing outpost for thousands of years. Paddling out in tule-reed canoes from what is now Marin County, the Indians camped at Ayala Cove and other spots to hunt deer and seals or to fish for the prolific runs of salmon through Raccoon Strait. They also hunted ducks and gathered acorns and other seed crops on the island.

In August 1775 Manuel de Ayala sailed his ship, the *San Carlos,* into San Francisco Bay and anchored at Ayala Cove. His main mission was to map San Francisco Bay for future Spanish exploration.

During the Civil War the federal government established Camp Reynolds in 1863 as a deterrent to Confederate sympathizers and to discourage possible use of San Francisco Bay by the Confederate Navy. Today the nineteenth-century military outpost is one of the island's most interesting places to explore. There is a parade ground for soldiers to muster, and a restored officers' cottage is staffed at times by spirited volunteer interpreters.

Gun batteries were placed on the Angel Island hills in the late nineteenth-century and further strengthened during World War I, when the island was used to house German seaman who were captured on ships in West Coast harbors. After Pearl Harbor Angel Island was intensely fortified because of the hysteria over a Japanese invasion. During the Cold War the island was a Nike missile base until 1963.

On the east side of Angel Island is an immigration station, constructed in 1905. Between 1905 and 1940 about 175,000 Chinese immigrants were processed through this station. The setting was not as uplifting as Ellis Island in New York, however, which welcomed immigrants. Immigrants detained on Angel Island were interrogated to see whether they met the qualifications for entry into the country at a time of general anti-Asian sentiment. Some were deported back to Asia.

Today you can tour Camp Reynolds and the Immigration Station to learn more details about Angel Island history.

A day on Angel Island is one of the most enjoyable outdoor experiences you can have in the San Francisco region. The views of the Golden Gate and the San Francisco skyline are outstanding. The level perimeter road can be walked or biked. Bikes can be readily rented in Tiburon or on Angel Island at Ayala Cove. A bus, called the TramTour, also operates continually on the island to take visitors around. The open-air tram tour includes recorded narration by people who participated in island history. Many visitors bring a picnic or buy lunch on the island and make a long day outing of the trip.

Getting there

Take a Blue and Gold Fleet ferry to either island from San Francisco's Pier 41 (415–773–1188). From late April to October the "Island Hop" ferry stops at both islands and includes Alcatraz's Cell House Tour and Angel Island's Tram Tour (415–705–5555). Another ferry service to Angel Island leaves from Tiburon (415–435–2131), crossing Raccoon Strait (named for an early British ship that stopped here). Call for the current ferry schedule.

Be sure to see

On Alcatraz be sure to tour the main cellblock, perhaps aided by an audio-cassette or ranger tour for explanation. On Angel Island walk, bike, or bus around the island to see Camp Reynolds on the west side and the Immigration Station on the east side.

Best time to visit

Warm and sunny times of the year are best for both islands. Angel Island's concessionaire services are most vigorous April to October. Alcatraz can be steep and slippery in blustery weather. The Bay is also more pleasant to cross in calm rather than rough weather. Other seasons are generally more congenial than winter.

Lodging

For a hotel with the feel of a B&B in the heart of the city, try the White Swan Inn (845 Bush Street, San Francisco, CA 94108; 415–775–1755; www.foursisters.com). With its dark wood paneling, rich floral carpets, and a fireplace in each room, the White Swan evokes the historic, small luxury hotels of London.

Dining

A restaurant steeped in detective literary history is John's Grill (63 Ellis Street; 415–986–3274). This landmark eatery was part of the setting for Dashiell Hammett's famous novel, *The Maltese Falcon*. Try the fresh seafood and shellfish, such as the fruits de mer pasta or the prawns and scallops en brochette.

For more information

Alcatraz Island tours can be reserved at (415) 773–1188. The Web site for Alcatraz, part of the Golden Gate National Recreation Area, is www.nps.gov/alcatraz.

The contact for Angel Island is Angel Island State Park (P.O. Box 318, Tiburon, CA 94920; 415–435–1915; www.angelisland.com). Ferries reach Angel Island from San Francisco (415–773–1188) or Tiburon (415–435–2131).

6

San Francisco Bay Area

Berkeley: Free Spirits and Free Speech at the University of California

In the 1960s Berkeley gained national media attention as the epicenter of the anti–Vietnam War and Free Speech movements. The times are less strident now, but Berkeley is still the intellectual and liberal political mecca of Northern California. Whether you see yourself as a retired revolutionary, a whiz-kid scholar, or a trendy culinary explorer, you'll find kindred spirits at Berkeley.

The historic story

In the 1960s Mario Savio spawned a Free Speech movement and protestors unhappy with the Vietnam War led an ongoing antiwar chant. As the sound bite–oriented, polarizing media of television sought its protester of the day, Berkeley—stronghold of both movements—was often the site of choice. Americans either loved or hated Berkeley, sometimes known as Berserkeley.

Today Berkeley carries on in a quieter manner as Oakland's cerebral counterpart and home of the University of California, the state's most prestigious public university. With its thousand-acre landscaped campus and scenic parklands, the university (founded in 1868) is the focus of most visits and invites a pleasant afternoon walk.

To enter the University walk across Bancroft at Telegraph and approach the Sather Gate. On your left is the Student Union, where you can get a free walking map of the campus at the Visitor Center (510–642–5215). Every Monday to Saturday at 10:00 A.M. (and 1:00 P.M. Sunday) there is a ninety-minute guided walking tour.

On your right, beyond Sather Gate, is the Sather Tower, popularly known as the Campanile, the major visual symbol of the university. For an impressive view of the East Bay, ride the elevator to the top of the campanile tower.

Be sure to check what's showing at the UC Berkeley Art Museum (2626 Bancroft Way; 510–642–0808) and the Pacific Film Archives (same building; 510–642–1124). The film library, the largest on the West Coast, shows special interest and esoteric films daily. The Phoebe Hearst Museum of Anthropology on the campus often hosts impressive shows of archaeological finds. The Bancroft Library displays a copy of Shakespeare's First Folio.

Around the campus extend the vital streets, pulsating with craftspeople, dreamers, and gourmet groupies. Telegraph Avenue, which extends from Sather Gate, is the most active of these streets, populated by students, artisans, and the homeless. Several coffee shops offer places to sip a cappuccino and watch the parade.

Shattuck Avenue, between Cedar and Rose, puts you in the heart of trendy Berkeley, close to the latest in gourmet grocery stores (Andronico's) and the landmark Alice Waters' Chez Panisse Restaurant (1517 Shattuck Avenue), which has probably had more historic influence on modern California cuisine than any other single establishment. Nearby is Easy Going travel bookstore (1385 Shattuck Avenue), one of the pioneering bookstores selling a huge selection of travel guides.

College Avenue extends from the university all the way to Oakland's Broadway. For the walker this is a pleasant stroll, with intermittent residential and shopping areas. The stores cluster around Ashby and from Alcatraz to Broadway, complete with several wine shops and specialty providers favored by carriage-trade gourmands. The Oliveto complex of restaurants and shops at the BART station on College Avenue is typical of the scene.

The University's Lawrence Hall of Science (510–642–5132), on Centennial Drive in the East Bay Hills, offers a quick immersion in the intricacies of science and technology. Built as a research facility for science education, the museum is filled with hands-on displays and exhibits where you can test scientific principles and conduct experiments. An astonishing Sunstone sculpture in back of the Lawrence Hall will alert you to the time of day and your place in the universe, provided that you ask for the brochure decoding the sculpture. If you are less ambitious, simply gaze out at the elaborate view of the East Bay from this promontory. The view from the Lawrence Hall and all along the Grizzly Peak Boulevard is one of the better vistas in the East Bay.

The Campanile has become a well-recognized symbol of the University.

As you drive up to the Lawrence Hall, you pass through Strawberry Canyon and the University Botanical Garden, which has 8,000 specimens of arid vegetation from around the world. Picnic tables in this garden and in the California Redwood section across the road offer places to relax.

Getting there

Berkeley is east of San Francisco across the Bay Bridge. Turn north on Interstate 880 and exit at University Avenue. Alternatively, take a BART train from San Francisco to the Central Berkeley exit. Enter the University where Bancroft meets Telegraph.

Be sure to see

Of all the Berkeley streets to peruse more thoroughly, Telegraph would be the first choice. Walk Telegraph Avenue from Bancroft to Dwight and then cross the street and walk back to the University. Telegraph Avenue is a kaleidoscope of humanity, a cluster of bookstores, and a collection of coffeeshops that invite lingering. Some months can be quiet on Telegraph, but as school starts in September and as the Christmas season arrives, Telegraph becomes a carnival of street vendors selling their crafts. Cody's (2454 Telegraph Avenue) and Moe's (2476 Telegraph Avenue) are the major bookstores. Cody's is the most complete store for new books, while Moe's, located on several floors, offers a large selection of used books. At Cafe Intermezzo, near the corner of Haste and Telegraph, you can nurse a latte.

Best time to visit

Any time of the year is good for a Berkeley visit.

Lodging

Gramma's Rose Garden Inn (2740 Telegraph Avenue, Berkeley, CA 94705; 510–549–2145; www.rosegardeninn.com), a large B&B inn in a converted 1905 Tudor-style house with a folksy atmosphere, is located a few blocks from the university.

Dining

Alice Waters' Chez Panisse Restaurant (1517 Shattuck Avenue; 510–548–5049) began a revolution in Northern California cuisine in the 1970s, emphasizing fresh ingredients and inventive cooking. The restaurant continues to flourish today.

For more information

Contact the Berkeley Convention & Visitors Bureau, 2015 Center Street, Berkeley, CA 94704; (800) 847–4823; www.visitberkeley.com.

7

San Francisco Bay Area

Oakland's Jack London Square:
The Literary Favorite Son

The call of the wild meets the call of the wallet in Jack London Square, a multiblock area of waterfront shops and restaurants struggling for identity even as the author did. Explore London's cabin from the Yukon and Heinold's Saloon—where London supposedly polished his literary skills—then enjoy an architectural tour through downtown Oakland.

The historic story

Oakland boasts a number of historic treasures, starting with Bay Area native son and literary luminary Jack London—one of the few persons around whom you could build a themed waterfront area. Popular attractions in Jack London Square include shopping at Cost Plus, book browsing at Barnes & Noble, and dining at Scott's, a fish-oriented restaurant.

At the Square you can view Jack London's cabin, said to be his Yukon abode from the winter of 1897–98. Next to the cabin quench your thirst at Heinold's First and Last Chance Saloon. Built in 1880 it is said that London acquired his self-made literary education at Heinold's. Inside you'll find Jack London photos and memorabilia.

In recent years Jack London Square has shown new vitality.

The lively nightspot in the Jack London area is the jazz club known as Yoshi's (510 Embarcadero West; 510–238–9200). Yoshi's also features Japanese dining.

A Sunday farmers' market draws large crowds looking for everything from specialty apples to goat cheese.

Jack London's cabin from the Yukon can be seen in Oakland's Jack London Square.

Franklin Roosevelt's Presidential Yacht, the *Potomac*, a National Historic Landmark, is now permanently berthed at Jack London Square. The public can sometimes tour the boat or participate in yacht excursions out on the bay. Call (510) 839–8256 for reservations.

A new Amtrak train station is the departure point for trips to Sacramento, Seattle, and Los Angeles. The Jack London Cinema features nine state-of-the-art theaters.

From the Square walk up Broadway into downtown Oakland. A civic group of volunteers sponsors free architectural walks around downtown Oakland. At Ninth Street, between Washington and Broadway, you'll see renovation and restoration in progress. This Old Oakland restoration consists of shops and restaurants, supplementing the excellent Ratto's international deli market and restaurant (821 Washington Street; 510–832–6503), a kind of culinary mirror of this diverse city. Around Old Oakland are new office buildings that have changed the face of downtown.

Farther up Broadway, at 2025, is the Paramount Theatre (510–465–6400), a lavishly gilded Art Deco movie palace from 1931.

West toward the freeways is another dramatic Oakland development, Preservation Park, Thirteenth and Martin Luther King, where sixteen early

Oakland Victorians have been gathered and restored. To complete your exploration of historic Oakland, be sure to see the Oakland Museum and Lake Merritt.

The Oakland Museum of California (1000 Oak Street; 510–238–2200) was one of the first museums to present environments, such as the American kitchen in the 1940s, rather than static collections, such as seashells of the world. Separate floors cover California art, California history, and nature in California. The second-floor Hall of California History presents a provocative look at the dreams and challenges of the Golden State. The museum architecture is noteworthy, with the building sunk into the ground and roof gardens atop each tiered floor. One of the popular annual shows is the mycological society's Fungus Fair in November, which displays the season's offerings in wild mushrooms.

Lake Merritt, a 155-acre saltwater lake in the heart of Oakland, is a popular recreation area. On the north shore of the lake lies Lakeside Park and the country's oldest waterfowl refuge, founded in 1870. You can rent sailboats, rowboats, and canoes at the boathouse on the west shore. Walking and jogging around the lake is popular, as are the free summer band concerts on Sunday at 2:00 P.M. Children enjoy the Fairyland amusement park with its fantasy rides and puppet shows.

Each spring 400 or so major artists, studio groups, and galleries throughout Oakland open their spaces for a weekend of celebration and public contact. The event, Open Studios, is arranged by a spirited arts group called Pro Arts (461 Ninth Street; 510–763–4361).

Along the edge of Lake Merritt, at 666 Bellevue Avenue, you'll find one of the outstanding public gardens in California, the Lakeside Park Garden Center (510–238–3208), covering 122 acres that are intensely cultivated throughout the year. Permanent displays include a Japanese Garden, Herb and Fragrance Garden, Cactus and Succulent Garden, Polynesian Garden, and a tropical conservatory. The chrysanthemum displays each autumn are famous, but specialized appreciators might single out a preference for the bonsai show each autumn or the dahlia root sale each spring. Aside from this Lakeside Garden area, both Oakland and Berkeley boast impressive public rose gardens.

Another historic lakefront attraction is the Camron-Stanford House (1418 Lakeside Drive; 510–444–1876). This restored Italianate Victorian was built in 1876 and was owned by the brother of Leland Stanford, railroad tycoon and university founder. The other premier area Victorian, in the Oakland Hills, is Dunsmuir House (2960 Peralta Oaks Court; 510–615–5555). Dunsmuir is a notable example of Victorian wealth and taste. Today it serves as a cultural, horticultural, and historical park open to the public.

Getting there

Oakland is east from San Francisco across the Bay Bridge. If you're driving, take the Broadway exit. BART trains can deposit you at the downtown Oakland Twelfth Street station.

Be sure to see

Jack London Square, Old Oakland, the Paramount Theatre, Preservation Park, the Oakland Museum, and details listed for Lake Merritt would be the sites to visit.

Best time to visit

Any time of the year is good for Oakland.

Lodging

If you're looking for an historic place to lodge in the region, try the Claremont Resort & Spa (41 Tunnel Road, Berkeley, CA 94705; 510–843–3000; www.claremontresort.com). This white fin de siècle palace of gentility has been recycled and repositioned by its owners as an "urban resort" with a spa.

Dining

The fish restaurant Scott's (2 Broadway; 510–444–3456) provides a waterfront view at Jack London Square. Try the fresh grilled fish of the day.

For more information

Contact the Oakland Convention and Visitors Bureau, 475 Fourteenth Street, Suite 120, Oakland, CA 94612; (510) 839–9000; www.oaklandcvb.com. The Jack London Square area has its own Web site at www.jacklondonsquare.com.

8

San Francisco Bay Area

Silicon Valley Origins: The Mission and Pueblo

From missions to microchips, Silicon Valley has been a premier stage for Northern California history. Get a sense of the distant past by visiting a replica of a mission church—and a feel for the nineteenth-century progress that presaged the future.

The historic story

Shortly after George Washington crossed the Delaware to do battle with the British in 1777, Padre Thomas de la Pena was planting a wooden cross on the banks of the Guadalupe River to establish Mission Santa Clara de Asis, honoring St. Clare of Assisi, founder of the Poor Clare Sisters and the first Franciscan nun. Settlement of the fertile Santa Clara Valley began with the founding of the mission and the pueblo of San Jose.

Today you can get a sense of the mission by visiting the University of Santa Clara to see its replica of one of the later mission churches. Then get a feel for the development of San Jose, especially as the nineteenth century progressed, in the downtown area. The Peralta Adobe records the Spanish-Mexican era, and the Fallon House portrays the early American period. Tiny Pellier Historic Park celebrates the development of fruit agriculture, especially the prune orchards. Begin at the mission, the eighth in the Franciscan chain. It is located on the campus of the present University of Santa Clara, off The Alameda in Santa Clara; (408) 554–4023.

Based on the Franciscan padres' own measure of success, Santa Clara exceeded every other mission in California. That criterion was, of course, the number of "heathens" baptized into Christianity, and 8,536 Native Americans passed through these rites at Santa Clara between 1777 and 1832. In 1800

The Peralta Adobe depicts life during the Spanish-Mexican period in San Jose.

there were 1,228 Indians associated with Mission Santa Clara—one of the largest concentrations of Indians in a mission at the time. Santa Clara also ranked fourth in total livestock among the missions in 1832, and every Saturday twelve cattle were butchered for the Indians' food.

The viceroy of Mexico envisioned Santa Clara as a perimeter supply post and fortification for Mission Dolores and Yerba Buena, the early name for the city of San Francisco. Santa Clara was to be the food-producing unit that would help sustain the regional Spanish presence. In this task the mission succeeded, assisted by the fertility of the soil, cooperation of the local Indians, and able leadership of gifted executives in the Franciscan order. The mission artisans were also well known, especially for their weaving.

On the campus today you see a replica of the third mission church, from 1825. Floods, earthquakes, fires, and inappropriate site choices damaged the earlier churches. Fragments of the original mission cross are preserved under glass in the current cross in front of the church.

An adobe wall from the 1822 mission period remains, along with an adobe structure that now serves as the faculty club. These adobes are the oldest buildings on a college campus in the western United States. Behind the adobe wall are olive trees, also from the 1820s. This peaceful, bloom-filled, enclosed area approximates for the visitor the calm, orderly garden compound of the early mission, with pealing bells marking the routine of the day. Bells from as early as 1798 still hang in the tower.

After perusing the mission, head for historic downtown San Jose.

In November 1777 sixty-six soldiers, settlers, and family members were chosen from the presidios at San Francisco and Monterey to found a new pueblo, San Jose de Guadalupe, at the south end of San Francisco Bay. The rationale for pueblos was to boost food production that could sustain the presidios and missions, institutions with which the Spanish had much experience in settling new territories.

San Jose grew slowly. By 1841 the population had risen from the original 66 to only about 300. Travelers commented that it was a small village with a few adobes and palisada, or tamped earth, houses. Life in San Jose was simple and primitive, yet the climate was attractive; retiring soldiers favored it for their homes. San Jose was a key point at the end of the immigrant trek from Sutter's Fort around the south end of San Francisco Bay, after the immigrants had crossed the Sierra Nevada. The Santa Clara Valley was often called the Valley of San Jose in those days. Later it received the affectionate name Valley of Heart's Delight because of the beauty of the fruit tree blossoms.

At 175 West St. John Street, near North San Pedro Street, you'll see the premier historic structure in the region, the Luis Maria Peralta Adobe (408–993–8182), the last vestige of El Pueblo de San Jose de Guadalupe. It was built before 1800 and later bought by Peralta, who had come to California with the Anza expedition in 1775–76.

Luis Maria Peralta and his wife, Maria Loreto Alviso, populated the countryside with seventeen children, a not uncommon number for Spanish families in California at that time. As a reward for military service, Peralta was given one of the largest and most valuable Spanish land grants, the 44,000-acre Rancho San Antonio. When he died in 1851 Peralta's net worth exceeded a million uninflated dollars.

In the twilight of the adobe era, excitement ran high as the Mexican War with the United States began in 1846. San Jose then had a public house and three or four small stores. Captain Thomas Fallon, whose later wooden house stands opposite the Peralta adobe, rode into town with his group of California Volunteers, captured the jail, and hoisted the American flag. Today the Fallon House (408–993–8182) is a museum showing artifacts of the period.

The most sustained economic life in this valley before the recent electronics boom was fruit agriculture, especially prune plums. Pellier Historical Park, at Terraine and West St. James Streets in San Jose, recognizes this contribution with plantings of plums, pears, and other orchard crops plus grapes, dedicated to individual pioneering agricultural families. The park is only a block from the Peralta Adobe.

The Romanesque-style post office building at 110 South Market Street has become the San Jose Museum of Art (408–294–2787). Though much of earlier downtown San Jose fell to the forces of modernization, this handsome old building was saved. Constructed in 1892 of locally quarried sandstone, this was the first federal building in San Jose. It served as a U.S. Post Office from 1892 to 1923. Designed by Willoughby Edbrooke, this is the last Romanesque-style structure on the West Coast.

Getting there

San Jose is 51 miles south of San Francisco on Highway 101.

Be sure to see

Make an itinerary of the Santa Clara Mission and then the San Jose sites mentioned (Peralta Adobe, Fallon House, Pellier Park, and San Jose Museum of Art).

Best time to visit

Any time of year is good for San Jose.

Lodging

A beautifully restored gem in San Jose is the Hotel de Anza (233 West Santa Clara Street, San Jose, CA 95113; 800–843–3700; www.hoteldeanza.com), dating back to 1931. The De Anza delights its guests with an Art Deco design.

Dining

The downtown French restaurant, Rue de Paris (19 North Market Street; 408–298–0704), features classic French cuisine. Try the pâté appetizer, the roast duck, and the almond torte desert.

For more information

Contact the San Jose Convention & Visitors Bureau at 333 West San Carlos Street, Suite 1000, San Jose, CA 95110; (888) 726–5673; www.sanjose.org.

9

San Francisco Bay Area

Sarah Winchester's Mystery House: An Urge to Build

Most people consult an architect when designing a home; it's said that Sarah Winchester consulted a medium. Is this 160-room mansion the result of an obsession with the spirit world—or an ostentatious monument to the material one? Visit and decide for yourself.

The historic story

The Winchester Mystery House is a Victorian extravaganza owned, designed, and built over thirty-eight years (1884–1922) by Sarah Winchester, heiress to the Winchester rifle fortune. Sarah built the 160-room mansion in San Jose—partly because she was obsessed with the process of building and partly because she had a disposable income of $1,000 a day (tax free until 1913). The house has beautiful details mixed with bizarre oddities, such as doors opening onto walls and stairs going nowhere. Many believe that Sarah was trying to communicate with the spirit world.

The story begins during the Civil War when Sarah Pardee met and married William Wirt Winchester, son of the manufacturer of the famous Winchester repeating rifle. Their one child, a daughter, died shortly after birth. William died fifteen years later. Sarah's inheritance was roughly $20,000,000 plus 48.8 percent of the shares of the Winchester Repeating Arms Company.

Sarah Winchester was deeply upset by these deaths. Beyond that, it is difficult to determine where the true story ends and legend begins.

It is said that Sarah consulted a medium, who explained that the spirits of all those who had been killed by the Winchester rifle had sought their revenge by taking the lives of her loved ones. The medium suggested that she could escape the curse by moving west, buying a house, and continuing to build onto it.

In 1884 Sarah moved to San Jose and purchased an eight-room farmhouse from a Dr. Caldwell. She then began her never-ceasing construction plan, building steadily, twenty-four hours a day, for thirty-eight years until her death.

She employed a small army of almost sixty carpenters, domestic servants, and gardeners to create the topsy-turvy project on her 161-acre estate. Certainly she was an eccentric. Whether she was in touch with some spiritual power and directed by that relationship is harder to determine. What is even more difficult to comprehend is Sarah's obsessions, such as with the number 13. There are thirteen coat hooks in the closets, thirteen windows in the rooms, thirteen steps in the staircases. There are also doors opening onto blank walls or dropoffs and staircases leading to dead ends. It is said that Sarah slept in a different bedroom every night.

The house is something of an architectural anomaly, roughly characterized as Victorian. The hardwood floors, elaborate trim work, and ornate gables are lovely. The Tiffany and other art glass in doors and windows is unsurpassed. The front doors to the house, installed in 1906, were of European art glass and were purchased then with $3,000 uninflated dollars. These doors are good examples of the masterpieces of detail in the structure. Twenty-four of the rooms are now outfitted with authentic Victorian furniture.

After the narrated house tour, which takes you through 110 of the 160 rooms, take a self-guided tour through the elaborate Victorian gardens. The gardens reflect the Victorian passion for collecting trees, shrubs, and flowers from all parts of the world. In fact, Sarah had plants on her estate from 110 countries. Her aviary was filled with tropical birds, which were kept warm year-round with a special heating mechanism. The garden tour takes you past major points of interest where a continuing tape narration tells the story. You'll see the estate greenhouse, garage, pumphouse, water tower, dehydrator, and gardener's tool shed.

The house deteriorated gradually after Sarah's death until 1973, when restoration began. In 1983 the house reopened as a museum with two additional resources, the Winchester Historical Firearms Museum and the Winchester Products Museum. On exhibit is the largest collection of Winchester rifles in the West. You'll see B. Tyler Henry's 1860 repeating rifle, which Oliver Winchester adapted and improved upon to produce his first Model 1866. The Winchester Model 1873 was a superior rifle with a steel mechanism and heavier center fire cartridges. It was this rifle that became known as

"The Gun That Won The West." Winchester made many other products, from camping equipment to bicycles, which are also on display.

Getting there

Winchester Mystery House is at 525 South Winchester Boulevard in San Jose. Winchester Boulevard is the first major road west of the intersection of Interstates 880 and 280. The Winchester Mystery House is .25 mile north of Interstate 280 on Winchester Boulevard.

Be sure to see

The tour at Winchester makes this site a destination in itself.

Best time to visit

Any time of the year is good for the Winchester Mystery House. Special Guided Flashlight Tours are given on each Friday the 13th and on selected Full Moon Nights.

Lodging

The luxurious Fairmont Hotel (170 South Market Street, San Jose, CA 95113; 408–998–1900; www.fairmont.com) is a gracious 541-room structure that anchors the restoration of modern San Jose. In few other cities could it be said that a hotel so energized the city's downtown.

Dining

The landmark Italian restaurant is still Original Joe's (corner of First and San Carlos Streets, 408–292–7030). There are 156 choices on its elaborate menu.

For more information

Contact the Winchester Mystery House, 525 South Winchester Boulevard, San Jose, CA 95128; (408) 247–2000; www.winchestermysteryhouse.com.

For area information contact the San Jose Convention & Visitors Bureau at 333 West San Carlos Street, Suite 1000, San Jose, CA 95110; (888) 726–5673; www.sanjose.org.

10

San Francisco Bay Area

Silicon Valley High-Tech Heritage: The Tech and Intel Museums

The computer revolution affecting America—indeed, most of the world—has changed the face of once-pastoral San Jose and what's now known as the Silicon Valley. Two innovative museums explore the legacy of the new-age pioneers who helped open this technological frontier.

The historic story

Originally a bucolic ranching region nurtured by a small pueblo and Spanish mission in the eighteenth century, the valley developed in the nineteenth and early twentieth centuries as one of the most important fruit-growing areas in America. Plums, apricots, peaches, and cherries were shipped all over the country from here.

At the end of World War II a new direction emerged—electronics and other high-technology industries—and San Jose began to grow. The area is now the eleventh-largest metropolitan region in the country, and the county has one of the highest per capita incomes in the United States. Computers, chips, and other high-tech products, both civilian and military, are the main manufacturing effort.

Two places celebrate the area's technical history: The Tech Museum of Innovation in San Jose and the Intel Museum, a few miles north in Santa Clara. The Tech Museum provides a broader interpretation of technology advances; the Intel Museum focuses on the chip and computer technology of this prominent company.

The Tech Museum celebrates inventiveness in several technical fields with more than 200 "minds-on" exhibits. Four themed galleries draw attention to technologies pioneered in the Silicon Valley:

Gallery 1, "Life Tech: The Human Machine," focuses on how technology saves lives and enhances human performance, as well as technology's social and ethical ramifications. One exhibit, Ultrasound Yourself, allows visitors to "see" inside themselves. After putting your hand in a water tank, you can see a cross-section of your hand and watch the bones wiggle on a monitor.

Gallery 2, "Innovation: Silicon Valley and Beyond," tells the story of Silicon Valley and the "revolutionaries" who made it famous with their inventions. One exhibit, The Miniature Revolution, allows visitors to enter a clean room area with working microchip fabrication equipment, the kind that has made Silicon Valley a major world center for designing and manufacturing advanced microchips and related devices.

Gallery 3, "Communications: Global Connections," celebrates the new information and communication technologies. One exhibit allows you to make a movie in the Digital Studio or see the latest feats in animation. Communication technologies on display show how they seem to make the modern world smaller and more connected.

Gallery 4, "Exploration: New Frontiers," takes visitors to places we have only begun to imagine. The Underwater Pilot exhibit uses remotely operated vehicles (ROVs) to investigate places where humans can't go.

Another aspect of The Tech is the Robert N. Noyce Center for Learning, named after the donor, a cofounder of Intel. The Noyce Center supports education in its effort to strengthen skills and encourage a deeper understanding of science, math, and technology.

As one might expect, The Tech exists both in a building in downtown San Jose and on the Web in a particularly lush and robust site, www.thetech.org.

The Tech is also the permanent home for an exhibit of the National Medal of Technology, the nation's highest honor for technological innovation. Established by Congress in 1980, the award was first presented by the president in 1985.

Another interesting perspective on the region can be gleaned with a stop at the Intel Museum. Intel is credited for many technical firsts in the development of computer chips. One was the first dynamic random access memory (DRAM). Another was the first erasable programmable read-only memory (EPROMS). Intel began assembling materials for the museum in the 1980s, opening it to the public in 1992 and expanding to a 10,000-square-foot facility in 1999.

The Intel Museum shows the technological evolution of the computer

The Intel Museum celebrates the history of computer chip
innovation from the 1960s to the present.

chip industry since the 1960s, inspiring wonder at the many developments that Intel has pioneered. Here you can see how computer chips are designed and manufactured. On a computer chip, millions of transistors are packed into a .25-inch square. The time that these transistors take to process information is measured in billionths of a second. The Intel Museum shows the differences between various kinds of computer chips.

The Intel Museum has more than thirty hands-on exhibits about the wonders of the computer and the chips that drive them. Visitors see how computer chips are constructed in ultraclean, highly automated factories and how chips pervade the products in our everyday lives.

There is a computer-equipped learning lab for digital storytelling and presentations on the Internet, art, science, and technology. Visitors are able to use computers in the museum to explore the Internet and try some of the latest in entertainment and educational software.

A technology-related gift store emphasizes such items as computer designs on apparel, jewelry with computer components, and "smart" computer-powered toys.

Getting there

San Jose and the Silicon Valley lie 30 to 50 miles south of San Francisco along the western and southern edge of San Francisco Bay. The Tech Museum is in downtown San Jose. Take Highway 101 south from San Francisco and exit at San Jose. The Intel Museum is north of San Jose in Santa Clara. Take Highway 101 north from San Jose, exit right on the Montague Expressway, then left onto Mission College Boulevard.

Be sure to see

The two museums present an interesting perspective on the modern high-tech revolution.

Best time to visit

Any time of the year is good for these two museums. Call ahead to verify times open.

Lodging

Another of the stately and historic downtown hotels in San Jose is the Hyatt Sainte Claire (302 South Market Street, San Jose, CA 95113; 408–295–2000; www.hyatt.com). The Sainte Claire was the venerable downtown hotel in the bucolic period before the modern Silicon Valley revolution.

Dining

For culinary daring that parallels the technical innovations of Silicon Valley, try Eulipia Restaurant (374 South First Street; 408–280–6161). The grilled trout is a specialty.

For more information

Contact the Tech Museum of Innovation at 201 South Market Street, San Jose, CA 95113; (408) 294–8324; www.thetech.org.

The Intel Museum is located at 2200 Mission College Boulevard in Santa Clara, CA 95052; (408) 765–0503; www.intel.com/go/museum.

The area contact is the San Jose Convention & Visitors Bureau (333 West San Carlos Street, Suite 1000, San Jose, CA 95110-2720; 408–295–9600 or 888–726–5673; www.sanjose.org).

11

San Francisco Bay Area

Leland Stanford's Farm: The Future University

Stanford University owes its existence to a tragic death. After typhoid fever took their only child, a fifteen-year-old son, Senator Leland Stanford and his wife, Jane, turned their 8,200-acre stock farm into the Leland Stanford Junior University so that "the children of California may be our children." You'll want to dedicate a full day to exploring the wonders of this lovely memorial.

The historic story

On October 1, 1891, Senator Leland and Jane Stanford officially opened Leland Stanford Junior University, which was destined to become one of the premier institutions of higher education and also one of the lovelier campuses in the West.

Stanford had used the grounds to raise prize racehorses, orchard crops, and wine grapes, and years later the cerebral establishment is still called "The Farm."

Starting modestly during the Gold Rush as a merchant in Sacramento, Leland Stanford managed to accumulate enough capital to become a partner in building the transcontinental railroad over the Sierra Nevada. The success of the railroad brought him prodigious wealth. Stanford rose in Republican Party circles and was elected governor of California.

Today's Stanford campus is home to 13,000 students. You can guide yourself with a map from Visitor Information in the lobby of Memorial Auditorium, opposite the Hoover Tower.

For the explorer, the first places to visit on the Stanford University grounds are the main quadrangle and Memorial Church; the Hoover Tower

Stanford's original architecture was modeled after the distinct Romanesque style.

with the Hoover Institution for War, Peace, and Revolution; and the Stanford University Museum of Art.

The most historic section of the Stanford campus is the original sand-stone quadrangle with its thick Romanesque features and Memorial Church. Distinctive in the university architecture are the enclosed courtyards, arch-ways, red tile roofs, thick walls, and buff sandstone from which the buildings are constructed. The dominant architectural model was the Romanesque style. There is a general feeling of unity, especially in the earlier buildings.

The primary architect for Stanford University was Charles Coolidge, but the clients, Leland and Jane Stanford, were far from passive. The Stanfords liked to participate in all details of the campus development. Because the Stanfords liked a certain Swiss hotel they had visited, a copy of that hotel was made to appear on campus as Encina Hall. Stanford hired the greatest land-scape architect of the day, Frederick Law Olmstead, but made it clear that Olmstead was his employee.

Leland Stanford conceived of the university as a physical plan more than as an intellectual monument. At his death in 1893 there was no clear allot-ment of the developing space for different faculties. His wife, Jane, and her brother, Ariel Lathrop, proceeded with the building but without the domi-nant force of the senator.

Memorial Church, dedicated in 1903, was Mrs. Stanford's memorial to her husband. The mosaics on the front were made in the Salviati Studio in Venice, Italy, and shipped to California. The church's tower toppled in the 1906 earthquake and was never rebuilt.

The 285-foot Hoover Tower offers a panoramic view of the surrounding region if you take the elevator ride to the top. Concerts using the thirty-five-bell carillon of Hoover Tower ring out at noon, at 5:00 P.M., and on special occasions.

The tower houses part of the Hoover Institution, which holds millions of papers and books related to world conflict. Included in the collection are the presidential papers of Herbert Hoover, Stanford's most celebrated graduate. Hoover wrote technical books on mining and directed mining operations in such distant locations as China. Some of the holdings are on permanent display at the base of the tower. The Herbert Hoover Room contains many documents from Hoover's boyhood, professional mining days, and presidency.

The Cantor Center for Visual Arts, formerly the Stanford Museum of Art, on Museum Way off Palm Drive, has an eclectic collection that includes much Stanford family memorabilia and the gold spike that united the first transcontinental railroad. Built in 1892 this is one of the oldest museums west of the Mississippi. Architecturally, the neoclassic building was the first to use reinforced concrete structural techniques; railroad rails served as the reinforcers.

The center/museum boasts an outstanding collection of Auguste Rodin sculptures. An outdoor sculpture garden off the west wing celebrates a Rodin sculpture collection second only to that of the Rodin Museum Garden in Paris. Other collections, ranging from antiquity to the present, include Oriental jade and ceramics, California landscape paintings, western Indian basketry and ceramics, ancient Near Eastern ceramic vessels, and an Egyptian mummy. One of the intriguing California contributions to the museum is a nineteenth-century Yurok Indian canoe carved from a single redwood log. Yuroks used these canoes on the Klamath River and in ocean trips to hunt sea lions.

Getting there

Stanford is 30 miles south of San Francisco, off Highway 101 at Palo Alto. Turn onto University Avenue. Continue straight on University Avenue until it crosses El Camino Real and becomes Palm Drive. Parking is available near the oval at the entrance to the campus.

Be sure to see

You can participate in various walking and golf-cart tours (650–723–2560). The tours leave from Visitor Information in the lobby of Memorial Auditorium, opposite Hoover Tower. The tours are usually led by students, who provide both youthful enthusiasm and an insider's knowledge of the current campus scene.

Best time to visit

Any time of year is good for seeing Stanford.

Lodging

Several converted Victorians in Palo Alto amount to pleasant bed-and-breakfast lodgings. Try the Cowper Inn at 705 Cowper, Palo Alto, CA 94301; (650) 327–4475; www.cowperinn.com. A Craftsman-style house, the Inn is an example of the early houses that formed what was called Professorville, the housing district for Stanford faculty in Palo Alto.

Dining

The most historic restaurant in Palo Alto is MacArthur Park (27 University Avenue; 650–321–9990). The ample, white-painted structure was a World War I hostess house, designed by Julia Morgan in 1918 for Camp Fremont in adjacent Menlo Park. Try the smoked baby back ribs or the mesquite-charcoaled swordfish.

For more information

Tours of the Stanford campus can be arranged by calling (650) 723–2560. The tour information is also on the Stanford Web site at www.stanford.edu; click on Visitor Information. Area contact is the Palo Alto Chamber of Commerce, 325 Forest Avenue; Palo Alto, CA 94301; (650) 324–3121; www.batnet.com\pacc.

San Francisco Bay Area

San Mateo Peninsula Bayside: Billy Ralston's Spirit and Eclectic Historic Gems

The pursuit of gold in Northern California led some to riches, but others found their wealth in the silver rush that followed. The spirit of Billy Ralston—who struck it rich as an investor in Nevada's Comstock Lode—is the best introduction to San Mateo County, the strip of land immediately south of San Francisco where many commuters still "live the good life" today.

The historic story

In the 1870s Billy Ralston became a symbol of the good life. He raced the train on horseback from San Francisco to Belmont, often beating the train with relays of mounts. At his fabulous Ralston Hall mansion in Belmont, he entertained notable travelers of the era with sumptuous feasts, setting a style for California hospitality.

Even Ralston's death was symbolic of his desire to live fully. After rigorous exercise, it was his custom to go swimming in chilly San Francisco Bay. One day he had a heart attack and drowned, or so the doctor said. The event coincided with the impending bankruptcy of the Ralston ventures because of changing and unfavorable business conditions.

Today you can go to the College of Notre Dame in Belmont (1500 Ralston Avenue), stand in front of Ralston Hall, and meditate on Billy Ralston, symbol of the good life on the peninsula. Then you can peruse an eclectic mix of historic sites in the area.

Beyond the Ralston House, several gems of historic discovery await you on the bay side of the San Mateo Peninsula.

The most fitting place to begin an exploration of peninsula history is on Sweeney Ridge, a 2-mile-long, 1,200-foot-high ridge above Skyline Drive in San Bruno. From Sweeney Ridge in 1769, Gaspar de Portola and his party became the first Europeans to see San Francisco Bay. Portola and his sixty-three men walked all the way from San Diego through the roadless wilderness to Sweeney Ridge, where they were confronted with a large body of water never before reported. For 200 years sailors had passed near the Golden Gate without discovering the bay. You can get up to Sweeney Ridge by driving on Skyline Boulevard to Skyline College, parking in Lot B, and ascending through the gate and up the winding gravel road to the ridge.

In coastal Pacifica visit the whitewashed Sanchez Adobe, (1000 Linda Mar Boulevard), completed in 1846 during the Mexican era. Today the adobe serves as a museum where the daily life of the early settlers is preserved. Call (650) 359–1462 for the current schedule.

The history of aviation in Northern California included many interesting firsts. San Francisco Bay was the first place where an airplane landed on a ship, envisioning the later grand era of the aircraft carrier. Northern California was also the first place where an airplane performed a loop-to-loop maneuver. To view memorabilia of these and other feats, peruse the aircraft, photos, and interpretive effort at the Hiller Aviation Museum (601 Skyway Road, San Carlos; 650–654–0200).

The San Mateo County Historical Museum offers an introduction to general area history. The museum is in the old Redwood City courthouse at 777 Hamilton Street (650–299–0104). A large reed canoe shows how the Ohlone Indian fishermen maneuvered in the bay and ocean. In 1777 the Ohlone population in the greater Bay Area was estimated at 9,000. An exhibit on the Mexican period details the trading pattern of Boston ships, whose captains sought cattle hides in exchange for such goods as tea, sugar, spices, and clothing. In the American period that followed the annexation of California, the lumber, oyster, whaling, and farming industries flourished here.

The Tripp Woodside Store, a general store opened in 1854, is now a museum housing many artifacts from the era. The history of the store and area rests on lumber, and inside you'll find the lumbering saws and oxen harnesses used when draft animals pulled logs down the mountain roads. The Tripp Woodside Store museum is meant to be a hands-on experience, so you can examine closely the bean sorter, apple press, scales, blacksmith tools, traps, and furs. Call ahead to check visiting hours (650–851–7615). The store is located at the corner of Kings Mountain and Tripp Roads in Woodside.

The Hiller Aviation Museum displays memorabilia of the first airplane experiments in the Bay Area.

The Filoli Estate in Woodside is a forty-three-room mansion with sixteen landscaped acres of gardens built 1916–19. This preserved home and gardens of William Bourn, heir to the Empire Gold Mine and head of the local water company, is one of the few grand houses from early-twentieth-century peninsula life now open to the public. The estate, on Canada Road, is open for guided tours; reservations required (650–364–2880).

Getting there

San Mateo's peninsula side is along Highway 101, immediately south of San Francisco. (See San Mateo Peninsula map on page 62.)

Be sure to see

Set up a driving itinerary that includes any of the mentioned stops: Ralston Mansion, San Mateo Historical Museum, Hiller Aviation Museum, Tripp Store in Woodside, Filoli Estate, Sweeney Ridge, and Sanchez Abode.

Best time to visit

Any time of year is good for San Mateo County.

Lodging

The bayside and coastside of San Mateo are close together, with the coastside the more interesting place for lodging and dining. For lodging try the Beach House Inn (4100 North Cabrillo Highway, Half Moon Bay, CA 94019; 650–712–3300; www.beach-house.com). Their oceanside rooms show the Princeton Harbor and a walking/jogging path along the water.

Dining

Also on the coastside, try the Moss Beach Distillery restaurant (Beach Way and Ocean Boulevard, Moss Beach; 650–728–5595). Coastal seafood is the specialty.

For more information

Contact the San Mateo County Convention and Visitors Bureau at 111 Anza Boulevard, Suite 410, Burlingame, CA 94010; (650) 348–7600; www. sanmateocountycvb.com.

13

San Francisco Bay Area

San Mateo Coastside: Shipwrecks and the Portuguese

The memory of historic shipwrecks and the lighthouses built to prevent further disasters highlight the drive along coastal San Mateo on Highway 1. When you grow tired of the seaward view, stop to explore the ethnic heritage of the coast's small towns and fishing villages.

The historic story

The San Mateo coast between the Montara and Pigeon Point lighthouses offers a bucolic seaside drive highlighted by beaches, farmland, and small coastal towns. Morning fogs tend to burn off by noon, so plan this as a late-morning/afternoon outing.

The road is relatively straight, compared with the roller-coaster rides possible along the coast north of San Francisco or in Big Sur, south of Monterey.

Pick up Highway 1 on the southwest side of San Francisco and drive south.

In Montara, stop at the Point Montara Lighthouse (650–728–7177). Turn toward the sea at Sixteenth Street, where you'll notice a small YOUTH HOSTEL sign. The lighthouse was built in 1875 after several major shipwrecks along this coast, first as a fog signal station with a deep whistle run by coal-generated steam power. Today the grounds are open to the public and the buildings function as a rustic all-ages hostel.

Proceeding south, watch the boats return to the fishing village of Princeton, and see what the sea has offered up as prizes. Several sportfishing charters leave from Princeton. Shops and restaurants offer seafood.

San Mateo Peninsula

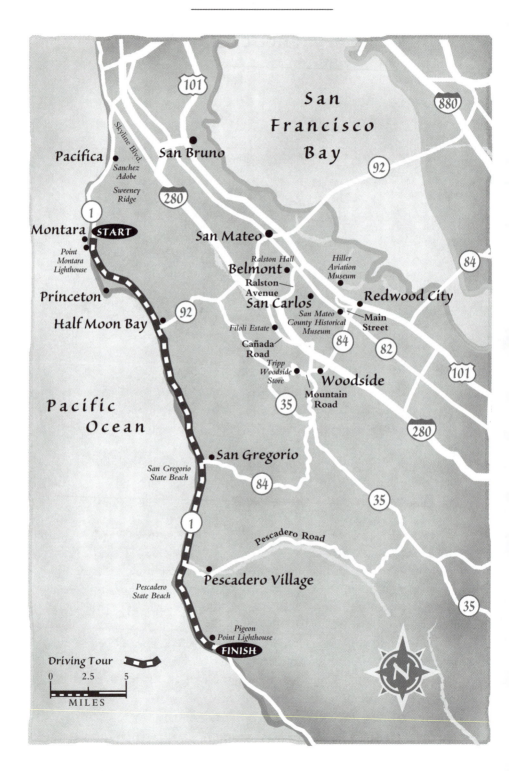

Next you'll encounter the original and main coastside community, Half Moon Bay, once called Spanishtown and populated by the Spanish as early as the 1830s. Today floriculture is big business here, managed in massive green-houses. Take a stroll on Main Street, where the blue Zaballa House (326 Main Street) is the oldest building. The Portuguese Zaballa family built the house in 1859 as the headquarters for their land grant in the area. The Zaballas opened the first market and saloon in Half Moon Bay.

The town of Half Moon Bay is compact and easy to explore on foot. As you walk along Main Street you'll see many historic buildings that have been carefully preserved. At 270 Main Street, the Greek Revival–style house from the 1860's was the home of Pablo Vasques, son of the original land grant owner.

At 448 Main Street, Cunha's is an old general store where Portuguese and Italian farmers often gather. Here you can buy everything from groceries to cowboy boots.

South of town, the landmark to see is the white Johnston House, poised on a hillside. It's amazing that this New England–style "saltbox" house could have been built in this roadless, isolated area in 1853. Hand-hewn timbers were floated ashore from ships at high tide. The setting exudes a certain long-ing, such as one feels in Andrew Wyeth's painting *Christina's World*.

Many beaches attract visitors south of Half Moon Bay, with San Gre-gorio and Pescadero among the most popular. The inland roads along the coast are also appealing. Drive inland south of Tunitas along Stage Road to the juncture of Stage and La Honda Roads, site of the Peterson & Alsford General Store, built in 1899. They sell everything from Levis to kerosene lamps, but mainly the establishment provides a friendly ambience for locals and visitors around its bar.

Proceed on Stage Road to the small community of Pescadero, which means "fisherman" in Spanish. When you drive the mile west to the sea from Pescadero, you pass Pescadero Marsh, one of the most important remaining habitats along the coast for bird life (180 species have been recorded here). Be sure to pack your binoculars.

Pigeon Point Lighthouse (650–879–0633), 5 miles south, is one of the major architectural legacies among lighthouses along the U.S. Pacific coast. Built in 1872, the brick structure, second-tallest lighthouse on the coast, is open on weekends. Wooden houses on the site function as an all-ages hostel, similar to Montara.

A generation of houses in nearby Pescadero were painted white after the SS *Columbia* wrecked here in 1896, floating landward its cargo of white paint. The importance of lighthouses along this treacherous coast can be seen in the

Pigeon Point Lighthouse is an architectural gem on the San Mateo coast.

place names. Franklin Point recalls that the clipper ship *Sir John Franklin* ran aground here with major loss of life.

The broad marine terraces along the San Mateo Coast present opportune agricultural benchlands that attracted early ethnic farmers. The land is not always exceedingly rich, but the climate provides a long, cool, fog-moistened growing season ideal for artichokes, brussel sprouts, and commercial flowers.

Getting there

Drive Coast Highway 1 south from San Francisco to enjoy coastside San Mateo.

Be sure to see

The best stops going south are the Montara Lighthouse, Half Moon Bay, Pescadero, and Pigeon Point Lighthouse.

Best time to visit

Half Moon Bay hosts several major festivals each year, including the Portuguese Chamarita Festival in June, the Coastside Country Fair on Fourth of July weekend, and the Art and Pumpkin Festival in October. Allow plenty of time to get there and back at festival time; the narrow roads can be jammed with visitors.

Lodging

San Benito House (356 Main Street, Half Moon Bay, CA 94019; 650–726–3425; www.sanbenitohouse.com) is a tasteful bed-and-breakfast establishment in an historic building.

Dining

Duarte's Tavern (650–879–0464) is a popular Portuguese restaurant in the one-street village of Pescadero. Try the cioppino or grilled fish of the day, followed by a dessert of local olallieberry pie.

For more information

Contact the Coastside Chamber of Commerce at 520 Kelly Avenue, Half Moon Bay, CA 94019; (650) 726–8380; www.halfmoonbaychamber.org.

Fort
Bragg

17

Willits

16 Mendocino

20

101

20

128

29 Clear
Lake

253

175

175

Point
Arena
Lighthouse

128

101

1

Pacific
Ocean

Fort Ross
State Historic
Park

15

116

To
Muir Woo

1

Point Reyes
National
Seashore

14

Train Tour

0   10   20

MILES

Drake's
Bay

Coast North of San Francisco

14

Coast North of San Francisco

Sir Francis Drake's Landing: Where in Point Reyes?

The precise spot on the Point Reyes coast where Sir Francis Drake landed his ship, the *Golden Hinde,* for repairs in 1579 remains a mystery. But your search for Drake can lead you to the glorious natural treasures of Marin County—including the San Andreas Fault and Muir Woods, a glorious stand of redwoods named, appropriately, after John Muir, father of the modern conservation movement.

The historic story

The more modern of the two historic stories involves legendary conservationist John Muir. When a benefactor in Marin County set aside redwoods in 1908, he decided to name the tract not after himself but in honor of the man who had dedicated his life to forest preservation, including founding the Sierra Club in 1892.

Muir Woods is a 560-acre sanctuary north and west of Sausalito along Highway 1. The holding is home to California's signature coast redwood trees, capable of living over a thousand years and rising 250 feet. Specimens of the same tree in the state's far northern region are the tallest trees on earth—a symbol of California superlatives.

Adjacent to Muir Woods and dominating Marin is 2,571-foot Mt. Tamalpais, one of the most agreeable hiking areas in the state and also one of the places where the modern sport of mountain biking was born. Trails range from shady paths deep within the forest to wide-open sunny strips running to the top of the mountain.

Point Reyes offers miles of breathtaking beachfront.

Farther up the west Marin coast is Point Reyes, "Point of the Kings" in Spanish, where Sir Frances Drake landed. Point Reyes is a designated National Seashore, where you can immerse yourself in several aspects of California history.

Presiding over all this is the haunting historic figure of Drake. Historians continue to write their dissertations arguing about the exact landing spot near what is now Drake's Bay. There is little doubt that the English swash-buckler put in his ship, the *Golden Hinde*, for repairs somewhere here in 1579. His ship was literally sinking with silver plundered from Spanish vessels. Drake was the first English explorer to land in North America, and though he claimed the land for England, the English never invested the manpower necessary to hold California as the Spanish did.

The road to Drake's Bay can be pointed out to the traveler at the Point Reyes Visitor Center, staffed by National Park professionals and spirited vol-unteers. Be on the lookout for what Drake called "a convenient and fit har-bor . . . with white cliffs and banks that lie toward the sea." Drake said that he nailed a brass plaque to a post to commemorate the occasion; finding that would be very special.

Two special historic walks close to the visitor center should not be missed before you pursue Drake: the walk to the re-created Miwok Village and the walk that illustrates the Earthquake of 1906.

The Miwok Village, Kule Loklo, comes alive especially when a Miwok descendant happens to be giving a demonstration. The Miwoks were a remarkable people, but because they left no tactile monuments, it is difficult to champion to the public their importance. They lived in a land of abun-dance at relative peace; it is sometimes said that their language had no word for war. The lives they pursued in their simple thatch houses, existing within the ecological means of their environment, is a quiet but eloquent lesson for all time.

The walk from the visitor center that illustrates the Earthquake of 1906 is also intriguing. Point Reyes experienced some of the most violent and lurching land shifts during that traumatic event. At one point along the walk is where a fence broke apart; the land offset is 16 feet. The Quake of 1906 continues to be referred to as The Great Earthquake, and if you have ever wondered what the Great Quake was like, this is the place to find out. The walk circles for a mile through meadows and bay laurel trees along the San Andreas Fault, with markers alerting you to the Pacific and American plates grinding past each other at roughly 2 inches per year. Along the Earthquake Walk you begin to imagine that Point Reyes is truly an island in time, des-tined one day to join the Aleutian chain off Alaska.

Getting there

The world of Muir, Drake, the Miwoks, and the Quake is easy to locate. Cross the Golden Gate on Highway 101, then turn west on Highway 1 to Muir Woods and beyond to Point Reyes.

Be sure to see

The cathedral of redwood at Muir Woods and the mysterious possibilities of Sir Francis Drake at Drake's Bay are worth exploring. Stop at the Point Reyes Visitor Center to get directions to Drake's Bay. Be sure to see the re-created Miwok Village and the 1906 Earthquake Walk near the visitor center.

Best time to visit

Muir Woods and Point Reyes are year-round destinations; they're good places in sun, fog, and rain. The mild weather is appreciated in all seasons.

Lodging

Sandy Cove Inn (12990 Sir Francis Drake Boulevard, Inverness, CA 94937; 415–669–2683; www.sandycove.com) is a restful lodging managed by proprietors aware of the historic treasures of Point Reyes.

Dining

The Station House Cafe (Main Street, Point Reyes Station; 415–663–1515) is an example of an old-line local favorite restaurant in West Marin; you can't go wrong ordering oysters from Charlie Johnson's Oyster Farm in Drake's Bay.

For more information

The local information source is the West Marin Chamber of Commerce, P.O. Box 1045, Point Reyes Station, CA 94956; (415) 663–9232; www.pointreyes.org.

For Muir Woods National Monument information, contact (415) 388–2595; www.nps.gov/muwo.

For Point Reyes National Seashore information, call (415) 663–1092, or visit www.nps.gov/pore.

15

Coast North of San Francisco

The Russian Incursion into California: Fort Ross

What a difference a few miles make! Had Russian colonists settled a little farther south, Russia might have played a much larger role in the history of California—and the United States. Ponder what might have been as you explore the historic reconstruction of a Russian outpost at Fort Ross State Historic Park.

The historic story

In its quest for furs, Russia established a North American beachhead at Sitka, Alaska, at the dawn of the nineteenth century. But Sitka was too far north for growing vegetables and wheat, so Russian explorers ventured by boat to California, where there were sea otters to be harvested and the hope of a more arable landscape to be farmed. The hope was unfounded, partly because the Russians settled a few miles too far north for the best farming.

The Russian colonial incursion into California occurred at what is now Fort Ross State Historic Park, on Highway 1 north of Jenner (707–847–3286).

The Russians established Fort Ross in 1812, landing with a party of twenty-five Russians and eighty Alaskan natives. They manned the outpost until 1841, when they sold the property to John Sutter of Sacramento, who transported whatever was valuable and portable to his own fort. None of the original buildings have survived; what you see today is a superb reconstruction, including the first Russian Orthodox chapel south of Alaska, the stockade, and the Commander's House, which contains exhibits on the Russian-American Company and the Russian occupation.

Be sure to allow plenty of time to peruse this Russian settlement, a gem

Fort Ross State Historic Park features superb reconstructions of the original outpost buildings that Russian explorers built in 1812.

of historic reconstruction and interpretation.

Before the Russians arrived the site was a village of the Kashaya Pomo Indians. According to one account the Russians purchased the land from the Indians for "three blankets, three pair of breeches, two axes, three hoes, and some beads. "At the time of settlement, Spain, France, and Great Britain were so involved in various wars that no one made an effort to challenge the Russians.

The structures were built of oak and fir using joinery technique common in maritime carpentry of the period. A wood palisade surrounded the site, as it appears today. There were two blockhouses, complete with cannons. Within the stockade were houses for the commander and officers, barracks for employees, and various storehouses. The chapel was built in 1824.

In the first years the hunt for sea otters was the primary pursuit. The pelts were extremely valuable in the China trade. Kodiak islanders from Alaska did most of the hunting using bidarkas (hunting kayaks) and atlatls (throwing sticks with darts).

By the 1820s hunting had so depleted the otters that agriculture and stock raising became more important. However, the coastal fog and rodent attacks on crops limited the settlement's agricultural success. Moreover, the

Russian men saw themselves primarily as hunters. By the 1830s the venture was becoming unprofitable and the Russians were ready to sell to the highest bidder.

Below the fort is Fort Ross Cove, the original sandy beach where the fur-gathering Russians landed and constructed ships. This beach, complete with a meandering stream, is a seldom-appreciated aspect of the impressive Fort Ross restoration. The Russians actually built four ships on this sandy beach between 1816 and 1824, using redwood and Douglas fir from the forests in the hills.

In 1873 the land was acquired by George W. Call, who organized the 15,000-acre Call Ranch. A wharf was built and a 180-foot chute was constructed from the bluff to slide lumber and bulk cargo onto ships anchored in the cove. Lumber, dairy products, vegetables, and fruit were shipped to the ready market in San Francisco.

Getting there

The fastest way to get to Fort Ross from San Francisco is to journey north to Santa Rosa on Highway 101, then west on Highways 12 and 116 to the coast at Jenner. Fort Ross is 11 miles north of Jenner on Highway 1.

Be sure to see

Fort Ross itself is the place to spend your time. A day could be absorbed in enjoying the many re-creations here, including a sealskin kayak such as the Alaskans in the Russians' employ used to harvest sea otters.

Best time to visit

Fort Ross is a viable outing any day of the year, but the Fort Ross Living History celebration during the final weekend of July would be the best time to visit. As many as 150 costumed participants gather, including some from Russia. Tall ships from various California ports come to the Fort Ross beach and fire their cannons in salute, with the fort firing back. Folkloric song and dance of the Russian period is also re-created.

Lodging

Fort Ross Lodge (20706 Coast Highway 1, Jenner, CA 95450; 707–847–3333; www.fortrosslodge.com) emphasizes a coastal environment with panoramic views. Some units have fireplaces and hot tubs.

Dining

For a commanding view overlooking the Russian River, magnificent at sunset, the place to dine in this area is River's End (11048 Coast Highway 1, Jenner; 707–865–2484). Try the local seafood specialties.

For more information

Contact Fort Ross State Historic Park at (707) 847–3286; www.cal-parks.ca.gov.

The local tourism source to the south is the West Marin Chamber of Commerce, P.O. Box 1045, Point Reyes Station, CA 94956; (415) 663–9332; www.pointreyes.org.

The tourism source to the north is the Fort Bragg-Mendocino Coast Chamber of Commerce, 332 North Main Street, Fort Bragg, CA 95437; (800) 726–2780; www.mendocinocoast.com.

16

Coast North of San Francisco

Art and the Gray Whale: The Town of Mendocino

The headlands west of Mendocino provide a particularly choice spot for viewing gray whales—natural wonders and one of California's ecological success stories. Head into town to view beauty of a different sort, created by the growing number of artists who show their wares at this picturesque seaside community.

The historic story

The story of the fall and subsequent rise of the California gray whale population represents an historic barometer of the state's ecological consciousness.

Infamous whaler Charles Scammons discovered that a certain lagoon in mid-Baja, Mexico, now known as Scammons Lagoon, was the birthing and mating point for most of the California gray whales. In an era when lamps were lit with whale oil, he slaughtered the whales after bottling up the entrance. After a precipitous decline of the species, the California gray whales have made a gradual comeback over decades to their current 30,000 numbers.

Watching (with the aid of binoculars) the whales swim south November to December past the Mendocino Headlands on their annual migration is a delight. The whales are moving deliberately from their Arctic summering grounds to their winter abode in warm Mexican waters. In March, when the whales swim north, the headlands are again an excellent place to spot these cetological treasures.

Beyond whales, the truly picturesque town of Mendocino is a pleasure to walk. Enjoy its historic seaside Victorian structures and the many artists who have congregated here because the traveler is also frequently an art buyer. Several of the grand earlier homes have become B&Bs and restaurants, such as MacCallum House and the Joshua Grindle Inn. One historic house from 1861 is now the Kelley House Museum (45007 Albion Street; 707–937–5791), with changing exhibits on regional history as well as a large collection of early California photos. William H. Kelley arrived here in 1852 at the start of the lumbering boom.

One further historic masterwork to consider is the magnificent 115-foot lighthouse at Point Arena (707–882–2777), immediately south of Manchester Beach. A light station was first constructed here in 1870, the result of a particularly disastrous night, November 20, 1865, when ten vessels ran aground here in heavy storms. The Great Earthquake of 1906 destroyed the original light station. Today's lighthouse, the same 115-foot height as the light at Pigeon Point in San Mateo County, is an architectural masterpiece. Point Arena ranks as one of the more photogenic of the lighthouses along the California coast and is definitely worth a tour. Climb the 146 steps to the top of this lighthouse and see the ingenious Fresnel lens that focused a small kerosene flame visible some 20 miles out to sea. On weekends the spirited citizens of the region act as docents at this lighthouse-museum.

How did Point Arena get its moniker? Captain George Vancouver spent the night of November 10, 1792, offshore in his ship *Discovery*. He called the place "Punta Barro de Arena" (point of sandy clay).

Outdoor pursuits at Mendocino might mean a hike to the Pygmy Forest, a canoe ride up Big River near Mendocino, or a bike trip into Russian Gulch State Park to a waterfall at the end of the trail.

The perhaps less visible historic story to celebrate in all this is the way California has saved its coast from development so that the land can be enjoyed for recreation and conservation by all people.

Getting there

The most direct route to Mendocino is to drive north from San Francisco on Highway 101, then west at Cloverdale on Highway 128 to the ocean, then north on Highway 1 to Mendocino.

Be sure to see

The Mendocino Headlands and the town are the main attractions. Start with the local art scene at the Mendocino Art Center (45200 Little Lake Street; 707–937–5818), which has two galleries and is the local mecca for art efforts. But the entire Mendocino coastal area is a treat to explore, with the historic Point Arena Lighthouse at the top of the list.

A whale sculpture graces the front yard of Mendocino's
MacCallum House Restaurant.

Best time to visit

Gray whales can be seen at Mendocino going south from early November through December. The northern journey occurs in March, time of the Whale Festival. Beyond the whale months, Mendocino is a year-round getaway destination.

Lodging

One of the stately lodgings along the coast is Stanford Inn By the Sea (Coast Highway 1 and Comptche-Ukiah Road, P.O. Box 487, Mendocino, CA 95460; 800–331–8884; www.stanfordinn.com). The inn runs a substantial organic farm. Hors d'oeuvres at wine time are vegetables from the garden.

Dining

Mendocino's MacCallum House Restaurant (45020 Albion Street; 707–937–5763) occupies one of the most historic buildings in the town. Outside, the carving of a gray whale from driftwood is a sculptural tour de force. Starters include grilled quail or field greens. The portabello mushroom or duck breast in tangerine sauce are tasty entrees.

For more information

The main tourism source is the Fort Bragg–Mendocino Coast Chamber of Commerce at 332 North Main Street, Fort Bragg, CA 95437; (800) 726–2780; www.mendocinocoast.com. When in town get information at the Ford House Visitor Center and Museum, 735 Main Street; (707) 937–5397.

17

Coast North of San Francisco

Riding the Skunk Train:
Fort Bragg to Willits

"You can smell 'em before you can see 'em," patrons once said of this train. The noxious coal engines—and the odor—are gone, but the railroad lives on. A ride on the Skunk Train and a visit to the Guest House Museum provide an engaging excursion into the history of the railroad and the lumber industry in Northern California.

The historic story

Small railroads played an important role in the historic development of Northern California. They carried products out, especially redwood lumber. They carried people when there were few roads. For those who lived along the railroad, the train was also the mail carrier. Today one of those railroads continues to flourish as an excursion train between Fort Bragg and Willits.

Fort Bragg, blue collar balance to Mendocino's artsiness, is known for its California Western Railroad, aka the Skunk Train.

While waiting to board the train, be sure to peruse memorabilia about the lumber industry and railroad in the Guest House Museum (707–961–2823) adjacent to the train depot. Historic photos of the train and the lumbering operation can put a traveler in an appropriately nostalgic mood for the trip. On display are copies of eight Carleton E. Watkins photos of the Mendocino Coast from 1860. The Guest House is a three-story Victorian from 1892, noted for the ornate woodwork in its interior, a typical Victorian flourish. Until 1912 the house was the home of C. R. Johnson, founder of the Union Lumber Company and Fort Bragg's first mayor. It became a city museum in 1984.

The Skunk makes a daily, narrated run inland along the Noyo River to Northspur. In summer the train proceeds with a further option, going on to Willits on Highway 101, 40 miles east of Fort Bragg. You can combine schedules and trains to suit yourself, getting on or off at Fort Bragg, Northspur, or Willits. Patrons ride in vintage 1935 M-300 motorcars pulled by ancient engines, including a noted "Ole' No. 45" Baldwin steam engine.

The train's destination, Willits, is named after early store owner Hiram Willits. The California Western Railroad station in Willits is a handsome and craftsmanly building made of redwood and cedar shingles.

While en route you can rest in enclosed cars if you wish or stand in open-air viewing cars, allowing for an intimate look at the redwoods and Douglas fir, the streams, wildflowers, grazing cattle, apple orchards, and occasional wildlife, especially deer. The train proceeds up Pudding Creek and the Noyo River, crossing thirty bridges and passing two tunnels on its way to Willits as you breathe in the fresh air of the redwood forest.

The half-day trip out to Northspur and back covers the western part of this scenic terrain.

The town of Fort Bragg is named after a fort begun here in 1857. The founder of the military post, Lieutenant Horatio Gates Gibson, named it in honor of a Mexican War hero, Colonel Braxton Bragg. The life of the fort was brief, only until 1867. Later, a lumber company took over the fort grounds.

Fort Bragg is a much less pretentious town than Mendocino, populated by lumber and fisher folk rather than artists and retirees. Main Street is indeed the major street in town. Noyo Harbor is popular for sportfishing and whale-watching excursions.

Anyone with an interest in California plants, especially the azaleas and rhododendrons of the redwood forests, will want to stop at the Mendocino Coast Botanical Gardens (707–964–4352), 2 miles south of town. The plantings cover forty-seven acres of coastal bluffs and can be explored with a self-guide trail map.

Getting there

The most direct route to Fort Bragg is to drive north from San Francisco on Highway 101 to Willits, then west on Highway 20 to the ocean. Fort Bragg is just north of the junction of Highway 20 and Coast Highway 1.

Be sure to see

The Skunk Train, at the foot of Laurel Street, and adjacent Guest House Museum are the historic highlights of this trip. The round-trip to Willits takes

*The Skunk Train makes its way through redwood forests on
its way to Northspur.*

seven and one-half hours and passes extensive redwood and Douglas fir
forests, crisscrossing the Noyo River.

Best time to visit

The Skunk Train operates year-round, but the summer schedule is more
extensive, traveling from Fort Bragg to Willits. The winter schedule is abbre-
viated, going only to Northspur and back. Call to verify train schedule.

Throughout the year the train offers special excursion trips, often in con-
junction with local festivals. In January there is a Crab and Wine Festival
lunch train. February brings a Presidents Day Special. Wine and chowder tastings in March are part of the Whale Festival. Mothers Day in May and
Fathers Day in June are big days for the train. There is a Wine Train tasting
special in May and a Beer Train in June. A Steam Train pulls the cars around
on Fourth of July weekend. A Halloween Train in October is guaranteed to
spook the young. Call for information on all of these events.

Lodging

One of the charming seaside destinations along the Mendocino coast is Heritage House Inn at Little River (5200 North Highway 1, Little River, CA 95456; 800–235–5885; www.heritagehouseinn.com). This large property has luxury rooms and some separate houses, plus a dining room with a view. Guests can walk the bluffs along the coast and enjoy a glass of wine with the sunset. Lodging includes dinner and full breakfast.

Dining

Breakfast and dinner are included with a stay at Heritage House.

For more information

Write or call ahead to confirm the train schedule. The contact is California Western Railroad, P.O. Box 907, Fort Bragg, CA 95437; (707) 964–6371; www.skunktrain.com.

For tourist information contact the Fort Bragg–Mendocino Coast Chamber of Commerce, 332 North Main Street, Fort Bragg, CA 95437; (800) 726–2780; www.mendocinocoast.com.

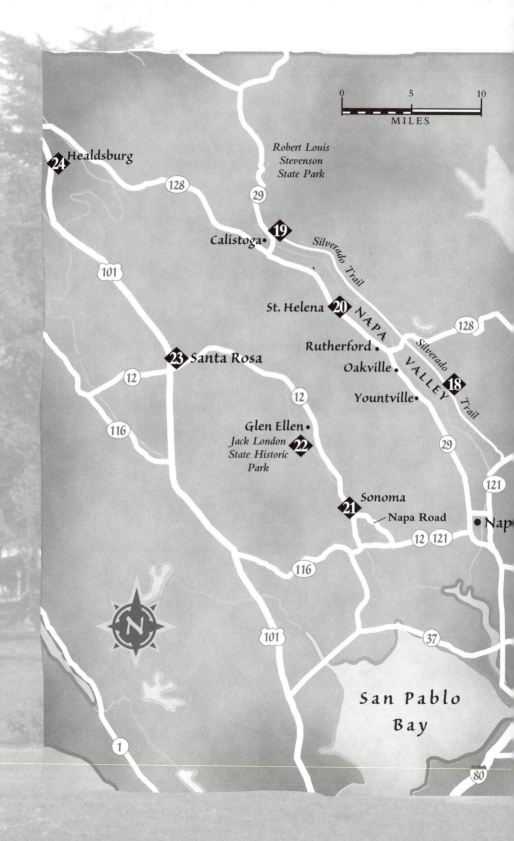

0   5   10
MILES

Healdsburg **24**

128

Robert Louis
Stevenson
State Park

29

Calistoga • **19**

Silverado Trail

101

St. Helena **20** N A P A

23 Santa Rosa

Rutherford •

12

Oakville •

Silverado

Yountville •

V A L L E Y

128

18

Trail

12

116

Glen Ellen •

Jack London
State Historic
Park

22

29

121

Sonoma

21

Napa Road

• Nap

12 121

N

116

101

37

1

San Pablo
Bay

80

Napa and Sonoma

18

Napa and Sonoma

A Passion for Cabernet: Napa Valley's Historic Wineries

Life is a cabernet—or at least it seems that way in the Napa Valley. Although the 240 wineries in the valley can make the choice of where to tour and taste a challenge, these three well-aged gems are sure to delight any traveler.

The historic story

Though many adventurers were drawn to California in search of gold nuggets, some discovered that the true gold lay in agriculture. No agricultural endeavor was pursued with more passion than the growing of grapes and making of wine, especially Cabernet in the Napa Valley.

Three wineries in the Napa Valley can be celebrated for their historic contribution to the development of California wine, their architectural significance, and their vital place in wine production today.

Niebaum-Coppola (Rutherford) was the creation of Finnish sea captain Gustave Niebaum, who arrived in 1876 and built a classic structure known as the Inglenook Chateau. The handsome brownstone building, covered with ivy, is an architectural treasure. Niebaum's wine goal was the production of rich Bordeaux-style Cabernets. In recent years movie director Francis Ford Coppola and his family purchased the winery, restored its wine-making reputation with the Coppola Diamond Series and Rubicon labels, and established a Parisian-style park and fountains in front of the winery for the public enjoyment. Inside, you can see memorabilia from the Niebaum era and from Coppola movie-making. There are two tasting rooms, one casual and one more formal. A store and cafe sell Coppola wine and food, mainly pasta and sauces. An elaborate tour and tasting is available at Niebaum-Coppola for a fee.

The great German Riesling wine-making traditions of the Rhine and Mosel River valleys contributed several pioneers to the Napa Valley. Foremost among these were the Beringer Brothers, who arrived in 1876 and built their palatial Rhine House and winery in St. Helena. The Rhine House is another outstanding architectural treasure of the Napa region. As was done in the Old Country, the Beringers dug caves deep into the limestone hills to provide a year-round, climate-controlled environment for their wines. (Wine stored in barrels in caves, which are high in humidity, do not lose much liquid through evaporation.) A cave visit is part of the tour at Beringer. The lawns, oak trees, and stately house at Beringer Vineyards make the scene inviting. Basic tour and tasting are complimentary; additional tasting of select wines is for a fee. Beringer puts emphasis on the white wine varietal of choice for the modern drinker, Chardonnay, but still also makes a Riesling.

The name Robert Mondavi is legendary in the modern era of the Napa Valley, that period since the 1960s when Americans once again learned to enjoy wine. The valley flourished with wine-making before Prohibition but was decimated when the Volstead Act of 1919 made wine-making illegal. The Great Experiment, as some called Prohibition, lasted from 1919 to 1933, and sons from a generation of wine families went into other businesses. A few families persisted, however, among them the Mondavis, holding their acreage together. There were 140 wineries in the Napa Valley in 1890, but only 25 in 1965. Robert Mondavi has been a tireless spokesman, promoting the joy of moderate wine drinking as an element of the good life. His Cliff May–designed winery, with echoes of California Mission architecture, is in Oakville. Basic tour and tasting is complimentary; a fee is charged for tasting the Reserve wines. Mondavi is especially respected for its big-flavored Cabernets.

For a pleasing outing drive north on Highway 29 and stop at all three wineries. Then turn east and drive south along the eastern side of the valley on the scenic Silverado Trail, where the rustic pleasure of the vineyard land-scape greets you.

Getting there

Drive north from San Francisco on either the west side of the bay on Highway 101 or the east side on Interstate 80. Depart from the major road to pick up Highway 29 and drive north through the Napa Valley.

Be sure to see

Traveling north along Highway 29, all three wineries are on the left side of the road. The first you'll encounter is the Robert Mondavi Winery at 7801

The Niebaum-Coppola Winery was founded by Napa Valley
wine pioneer Gustave Niebaum.

St. Helena Highway (Highway 29), Oakville (707–259–9463; www.
robertmondavi.com). Next comes the Niebaum-Coppola Winery, 1991 St.
Helena Highway, Rutherford (707–968–1100; www.niebaum-coppola.com).
Finally you'll see Beringer Vineyards on St. Helena Highway, St. Helena
(707–963–7115, www.beringer.com). North of Beringer, turn east on any
side road, then drive south on the Silverado Trail to savor vineyards far from
the traffic and development along Highway 29. Napa Valley wineries are open
roughly 10:00 A.M. to 5:00 P.M. seven days a week; hours are sometimes
longer in summer, shorter in winter.

Best time to visit

Any time of the year is good, but September and October are especially
pleasing. The bustle of the grape harvest is under way, and the vine leaves are
changing from shades of green to flaming reds and yellows. Autumn is almost
as popular as summer, the peak travel time, so travelers desiring the quietest
period visit here during the Mustard Festival, February to April, when the
fields are colorful with wild mustard and many musical and art events are
scheduled.

Lodging

The city of Napa enjoyed a bucolic Victorian gentility at the turn of the century. Some of the great houses built at that time have become B&Bs today. One example is the Beazley House (1910 First Street, Napa, CA 94559; 800–559–1649; www.beazleyhouse.com) with its half acre of lawns and tranquil gardens.

Dining

Try the Wine Spectator Greystone Restaurant in the Culinary Institute of America at Greystone (2555 Main Street, St. Helena; 707–967–1010). The restaurant is located in a massive stone structure from 1889 known as Greystone, one of the largest stone buildings in the world. Originally envisioned as a cooperative winery by its creator, William Bourn, Greystone flourished from 1950 to 1989 as a Christian Brothers winery. Try the Chef's Tastings plate as an appetizer, perhaps followed by the grilled Pacific tuna.

For more information

Contact the Napa Valley Conference & Visitors Bureau at 1310 Napa Town Center, Napa, CA 94559; (707) 226–7459; www.napavalley.com.

19

Napa and Sonoma

The Visionary of Calistoga: Sam Brannan's Hot Springs

Soak up some history as you trace the footsteps of spa entrepreneur Sam Brannan at the Sharpsteen Museum.

The historic story

Sam Brannan envisioned a resort at Calistoga in the north end of the Napa Valley as early as 1852. He pushed through a railroad spur to the area, only 75 miles from San Francisco, so that journeying there would be easy.

What does Calistoga mean, anyway? The story of the naming of the area is amusing. Brannan liked the wine and brandy of the Napa Valley as well as the hot springs. One day, after drinking a few glasses of this liquid sunshine, he found himself in a social situation and proposed a toast. Thinking of the other great hot springs resort area in the United States, Saratoga, New York, Brannan attempted to say that he wanted his resort area to "be the Saratoga of California." But Brannan's tongue was not as nimble as he might have wished that day, and his words came out as "be the Calistoga of Sarafornia." Those who heard the toast wouldn't let him forget it, and the name Calistoga stuck.

At the Sharpsteen Museum you can see a diorama presenting Brannan's grand vision of his Calistoga Hot Springs Township, which had a hotel and thirteen cottages plus a racetrack. Brannan, who owned 2,000 acres in the area, had visions of starting a silk industry and raising Merino sheep, but these plans failed. Part of the Sharpsteen Museum is in one of Brannan's original cottages, filled with a piano, bed, and chest of drawers from his day.

Beyond the Sharpsteen Museum, some interesting things to do here are visit Faithful Geyser on Tubbs Road and then soak in hot water or take spa mud treatments, as Brannan would have encouraged.

The Faithful Geyser is indeed faithful. Geothermal activity under Calistoga is so predictable that the geyser spouts into the air at regular intervals, though the times vary with the amount of ground moisture. Proprietor Olga Kolbek has watched the geyser since 1971. This geyser, said to be one of only three faithful gesyers in the world, spews forth 350-degree water roughly every twenty minutes on a predictable timetable, shooting a 30-foot plume of steam into the air. When the geyser pattern becomes irregular, there is a good chance of a regional earthquake in the works, a correlation that becomes documented more thoroughly with each major quake. The entire region has much geothermal activity, with electrical generation taking place to the north at The Geysers, one of the world's largest geothermal electrical production sites.

Some thirteen spas provide many opportunities to soak in hot water or take mud bath treatments in Calistoga. A "the works" treatment might involve a hot mud pack, hot mineral bath, towel wrap, and massage. Some of the lodgings, such as Carlin Country Cottages, have natural hot water piped into hot tubs in their rooms. Indian Springs Resort has a large outdoor pool of hot water, available to people who lodge and spa with them.

The town of Calistoga is one of the most enjoyable small towns in Northern California to explore. The people are friendly in this one-street egalitarian town. The main street is also located off Highway 29, unlike St. Helena, so there is peace and quiet. The town has a bookstore, a brewpub, and several fine restaurants.

Getting there

Calistoga is at the northern end of the Napa Valley, beyond St. Helena. Drive north on Highway 29 and exit east into Calistoga. Reach the Napa region by driving north from San Francisco on either the west side of the bay on Highway 101 or the east side on Interstate 80.

Be sure to see

Everything in Calistoga is within easy walking distance. The Sharpsteen Museum (707–942–5911), staffed by volunteers, shows many Brannan-era artifacts and is generally open 10:00 A.M. to 4:00 P.M. Faithful Geyser is at 1299 Tubbs Road; call (707) 942–6463.

*Calistoga's Sharpsteen Museum features many
mid-nineteenth-century artifacts.*

Best time to visit

Any time of year is good for Calistoga. The town gets busy in summer and autumn; winter months are very quiet.

Lodging

At Carlin Country Cottages (1623 Lake Street, Calistoga, CA 94515; 707–942–9102; www.carlincottages.com), hot water from the thermal underground source is piped right into the hot tub in your room. A central hot swimming pool and tub is open to all guests. There are fifteen comfortable motel–type rooms with refrigerators to chill down a bottle of Chardonnay or store picnic fixings.

Dining

Calistoga is known for its unpretentious good food and service. The All Seasons Cafe (1400 Lincoln Avenue; 707–942–9111) is one example. Try the cafe-smoked salmon or the grilled rabbit with a mustard glaze. Wines purchased from the restaurant wine shop are served at the economical retail price.

For more information

Contact the Calistoga Chamber of Commerce at 1458 Lincoln Avenue, Calistoga, CA 94515; (707) 942–6333; www.calistogafun.com. The overall area tourism source is the Napa Valley Conference & Visitors Bureau, 1310 Napa Town Center, Napa, CA 94559; (707) 226–7459; www.napavalley.com.

20

Napa and Sonoma

"The Wine Is Bottled Poetry": Robert Louis Stevenson in the Napa Valley

One of the most engaging early books about nineteenth-century California is *The Silverado Squatters,* Robert Louis Stevenson's account of his 1880 visit to the Napa Valley. Get the full story of his wanderings at the Robert Louis Stevenson Museum in St. Helena, then hike to where the emerging writer honeymooned and recorded his impressions of the area.

The historic story

Among the more felicitous phrases that Robert Louis Stevenson (1850–1894) used to describe the Napa Valley was his assessment that "the wine is bottled poetry."

A stop at the Robert Louis Stevenson Museum in St. Helena can acquaint you with the full story of his wanderings here. Over 8,000 artifacts of Stevensoniana, including first editions, original letters, and manuscripts, can be savored. Stevenson was the author of such classics as *Treasure Island, Dr. Jekyll and Mr. Hyde,* and *A Child's Garden of Verse,* and the locations in *Treasure Island* were directly affected by his observations in Napa. At the museum you can see many endearing artifacts of Stevenson, including the toy soldiers that he played with as a boy.

In the 1880s the Napa Valley, roughly 35 miles from Carneros to Mt. St. Helena, already was producing outstanding wine and captivating visitors with its classic valley proportions. An observer named Frona Waite wrote a book on California viticulture of the time, which will amaze a modern reader with its detail on how developed wine production was then.

Earlier, shortly after the Gold Rush of 1848, the Napa Valley was planted totally in wheat. In 1848 flour sold for 1½ cents a pound, but in 1850, with thousands of miners in California, flour was worth $1.50 a pound. The Bale Grist Mill State Historic Park in the Napa Valley tells this previticulture part of the Napa Story.

A taste of sparkling wine at Shramsberg Winery can repeat Stevenson's tasting at this winery, an early maker of champagnes, as sparkling wines were then called. Stevenson tasted about fifteen champagnes with the proprietor of Schramsberg, which suggests how advanced California wine production was even at that early time. Today you can see the original owner's house and taste wine in the caves, but call ahead for an appointment.

A hike to Stevenson's cabin site, now Robert Louis Stevenson State Park, completes the outing. A trail proceeds a mile up the mountain to where the author stayed in an abandoned cabin at a defunct silver mine, the Silverado Mine. Nothing remains of the cabin today, but at the site is a marble book on a pedestal, with some of Stevenson's poetry inscribed. Here Stevenson hoped that the dry air would help him regain his health, which was frail due to a bronchial congestion. He delighted in his marriage to Fannie Van de G. Osbourne, hoping his family would approve and continue his funding, and he began writing some of the early works that launched his literary career. The hike to the former cabin site requires that you be in good condition; there are picnic tables at the base of the trail.

The terrain of the park beyond the cabin comprises 4 miles along an ascending fire road to the top of Mt. St Helena. The view from the top ranks among the finest views in Northern California. On a clear day you can see San Francisco and Mt. Tamalpias to the south, the Sierras to the east, Mt. Lassen and Mt. Shasta to the north, and the Pacific Ocean to the west. The hike requires that you be fit and take plenty of water and protective gear for rain, wind, or hot sun. There are evergreen forests in the canyons and on the north slopes. In this sunny inland area, the south-facing slopes are dry chapparal.

Getting there

Drive north in the Napa Valley on Highway 29 to St. Helena, where you will find the Silverado Museum. Schramsberg Winery is west of Highway 29 between St. Helena and Calistoga. Robert Louis Stevenson State Park is 8 miles north of Calistoga on Highway 29 en route to Clear Lake. For a further enjoyable drive that approximates the bucolic beauty of Stevenson's period,

Visit the historic Schramsberg Winery where Robert Louis Stevenson enjoyed tasting Napa Valley's sparkling wines.

drive south along the Silverado Trail from Calistoga to Napa on the east side of the Napa Valley.

Be sure to see

The Silverado Museum (1490 Library Lane, St. Helena; 707–963–3757) is the critical first stop. You might want to purchase a reprint copy of *The Silverado Squatters*. Schramsberg Winery is west of Highway 29 in Calistoga. Call ahead (707–942–4558) for touring and tasting appointments. The undeveloped state park dedicated to Stevenson (707–942–4575), which has the hiking trail to his former cabin site, is 8 miles north of Calistoga on Highway 29. Park at the historic trailhead and picnic tables shortly after you see the park sign.

Hike west 1 mile to the cabin site and continue another 4 miles if you want to reach the top of Mt. St. Helena. Back in the valley, the Bale Grist Mill is in Bothe-Napa State Park on Highway 29 (3601 St. Helena Highway; 707–942–4575). Bale Grist Mill presents an interesting living-history look at the wheat flour world of Napa before wine. Find information on both the Stevenson and Bale Grist Mill parks at www.cal-parks.ca.gov.

Best time to visit

The Napa Valley is engaging any time of the year. Hiking through Stevenson State Park is idyllic in late autumn and winter during a sunny period after the rains have cooled the area. In late spring the ground is still moist and wildflowers are abundant. Summer can be hot and dry. Winter is the quietest time for tasting at Schramsberg.

Lodging

Calistoga's Indian Springs Resort (1712 Lincoln Avenue, Calistoga, CA 94515; 707–942–4913; www.indianspringscalistoga.com) has lodgings with kitchens and ample lawns, a large outdoor hot pool, and a full-service spa on the property. The lodging is only a short walk from downtown Calistoga's restaurants, shops, and grocery markets. The waters at Indian Springs—containing one of the largest natural hot springs in the region—were used by the Native Californians. The springs were a major factor in the early positioning of Calistoga as a spa resort in the nineteenth century.

Dining

Piatti, (6480 Washington Street, Yountville; 707–944–2070) is one of the classic, established restaurants of the Napa Valley. Their signature sweetbreads, roasted portabello mushroom pasta, and wood-oven roasted duck breast draw many of the local winemakers as repeat customers.

For more information

Contact the St. Helena Chamber of Commerce at 1010 Main Street, St. Helena, CA 94574; (800) 799–6456; www.sthelena.com. Also contact the area's overall tourism source, the Napa Valley Conference & Visitors Bureau, 1310 Napa Town Center, Napa, CA 94559; (707) 226–7459; www.napavalley.com.

21

Napa and Sonoma

Mariano Vallejo's Hospitality: The Sonoma Town Square

In the transition from Mexican to American rule in California, the presence of Mariano Vallejo of Sonoma looms large. Vallejo was skillful enough to flourish under both regimes. A short walk from the town square takes you to the home where he set a pattern for hospitality that has become a mark of the open California lifestyle.

The historic story

Sonoma was the most northerly reach of Spanish/Mexican penetration in California. The mission and adjacent military post were founded here at a time when friction between Spain and Mexico escalated, so the resources for founding missions diminished.

Outside influences were also affecting California, including the Boston whaling ships that Richard Henry Dana describes is his book *Two Years Before the Mast*. Overland treks of the first mountain men/explorers, such as Jedediah Smith, brought another element of change to the mix.

The Sonoma Mission, the barracks where soldiers were stationed, the town square, and Mariano Vallejo's house make intriguing stops in Sonoma.

The mission church, named San Francisco Solano de Sonoma, is a stark, white, low-slung structure, less elaborate and more of an outpost than were the other missions farther south. Father Jose Altimira, who was ambitious and talented, founded the mission in 1823, but he was a generation too late to expand the mission system. This twenty-first mission was destined to be the last Franciscan venture in California. The mission now houses the Jorgensen

Collection, a special collection of paintings of the missions.

The barracks is where the soldiers stationed at Sonoma stowed their gear and horses.

The town square of Sonoma, one of the prettiest in Northern California, is as close to bucolic picturesque as you will find. Huge old oak trees stand at attention over the grass and gardens. There are over a dozen buildings around the square dating from 1823 to 1855. One of the interesting monuments in the square is to the Bear Flag Patriots, a revolt that was a curious moment in California history. The year was 1846, and the future of California was a guessing game. Would the area remain under Mexican control? Would the United States extend its Manifest Destiny domination to this western shore? Or would California become its own republic? Some hotheads in Sonoma, favoring the republic idea, fashioned a crude flag with a bear on it, which looked more like a pig, and hoisted their Bear Flag in honor of the California Republic. The movement was swept away twenty-five days later when an American naval vessel captured Monterey, the Mexican capital. The Gold Rush events of 1848 confirmed the political direction of the area, bringing a stampede of Americans and ensuring that California would be part of the United States—though it was touch and go for a while whether California would be admitted as a Northern or a Southern state.

Mariano Vallejo's house, a short walk from the square, is a New England Gothic–style structure from the American period of his life. Called Lachryma Montis, or Tears of the Mountain, after the numerous springs in the hillside, Vallejo's house is an interesting expression of house construction at the time. It was built in 1851 as a totally prefab house fashioned in New England of spruce wood and then shipped around Cape Horn to California. Many touches of rural aristocratic life are evident in the furnishings. Vallejo lived here until his death in 1890.

While in Sonoma, appreciators of California wine history might enjoy a stop at the Buena Vista Winery, the original home of Colonel Agoston Haraszthy. Haraszthy is often cited as "The Father of California Wine." He brought the select and noble vinifera varietal cuttings from Europe to replace the so-called Mission grapes planted by the Franciscan fathers. Mission grapes produced a wine satisfactory for sacramental purposes but not very interesting for purely secular gustatory satisfaction. Haraszthy founded Buena Vista in 1857. The other notable historic winery within walking distance in Sonoma is Sebastiani, which has been a family affair for generations.

Getting there

Drive north from the Bay Area on either Highway 101 or Interstate 880.

Mariano Vallejo's house is a New England Gothic–style structure from the American period of his life.

Take the smaller Highway 116 or 121 until you reach the junction with Highway 12, then drive north on Highway 12 into Sonoma.

Be sure to see

The Sonoma Mission is part of a state historic park at the edge of the square, 20 East Spain Street (707–938–9560; www.cal-parks.ca.gov). Adjacent is the barracks, also on the edge of the square. Spend some time enjoying the square, with its Bear Flag statue, and its many restaurants, shops, small hotels, and a famous deli—The Sonoma Cheese Factory, 2 Spain Street; (800) 535–2855—where jack cheese is made and every conceivable picnic item is purchasable. Vallejo's house (707–938–9559) is a half-mile northwest of the plaza. The Buena Vista Winery (707–938–1266) is at 18000 Old Winery Road, near the square. Sebastiani Winery (707–938–5532) is at 389 Fourth Street East.

Best time to visit

Sonoma is an excellent year-round destination. The outlying areas reflect the agricultural seasons.

Lodging

Sonoma Mission Inn and Spa (18140 Highway 12, Sonoma, CA 95476; 800–862–4945; www.sonomamissioninn.com) is the dominant lodging in the Sonoma area, built around an elaborate hot springs and spa. The Spa offers a wide range of treatments. The Sonoma Mission Inn and Spa is one of the most historic properties in Northern California. As early as the 1840s, eccentric San Francisco physician Dr. T. M. Leavenworth was developing the property's hot water springs as a commercial healing spa.

Dining

The Depot Hotel–Cucina Rustica (241 First Street West, Sonoma; 707–938–2980), a restaurant in an 1870s building 1 block north of the plaza, features "rustic Northern Italian cuisine," as its name applies.

For more information

The overall Sonoma tourism resource is the Sonoma County Tourism Program, 520 Mendocino Avenue #210, Santa Rosa, CA 95401; (800) 576–6662; www.sonomacounty.com. The town of Sonoma is more directly represented by the Sonoma Valley Visitors Bureau, 453 First Street East, Sonoma, CA 95476; (707) 996–1090; www.sonomavalley.com.

22

Napa and Sonoma

The Socialist as Literary Entrepreneur: Jack London's Valley of the Moon

Ponder the tragic life and times of native son Jack London at the author's gravesite and charred ruins of his Wolf House retreat in an area of Sonoma he called The Valley of the Moon.

The historic story

Jack London achieved fame with his Arctic tales, most notably *Call of the Wild* (1903), but he also wrote gritty reports about growing up in Oakland, such as his novel *Martin Eden*. Tragedy dogged Jack London's life, ultimately ending it far too early. One of the tragedies was the accidental burning in 1913 of his handsome Wolf House retreat in Glen Ellen in the Sonoma Valley. London lived in Glen Ellen from 1905 until his death in 1916.

At the visitor center artifacts tell the story of bootstrapping London, who worked his way up from a kid robbing oyster beds in Oakland to author with international fame. The visitor center was built by London's widow, Charmian, who lived here and called it the House of Happy Walls until her death in 1955. Today the visitor center functions as a museum to London's Alaska and South Seas adventures. Appreciators of London can see original editions of his works.

Aspiring authors can peruse some of the 600 rejection slips that London received before he became famous, at which point editors were tripping over themselves to get him to contribute something—anything—to their periodicals.

The most poignant artifact of all is a 1916 newsreel of this gifted and relatively young man filmed a few days before his death. London died young of kidney failure, partly induced by his alcoholic excesses.

For London, the Valley of the Moon was a retreat. "When I first came here, tired of cities and people, I settled down on some of the most beautiful, primitive land to be found in California," he wrote.

London was a paradoxical man with many sensibilities. His man-against-the-elements tales brought him fame. He was an entrepreneur but also a socialist. He is famous for the life statement, "I would rather be a superb meteor, every atom of me in magnificent glow, than a sleepy and permanent planet."

The state historic park now comprises 800 acres and has ample hiking trails for the traveler who wants to enjoy the rolling oak-and-grassland hill country that is a signature of Northern California geography. The current park is part of the author's original 1,500-acre ranch, which he called Beauty Ranch.

London's legacy has been nurtured by Winnie Kingman and her late husband, Russ Kingman, at their Jack London Bookstore in the nearby town of Glen Ellen. They published an appreciative volume, *A Pictoral Life of Jack London,* and have collected most of his first editions. Be sure to stop by this store after visiting the park.

In his final years the energetic London was an active agricultural experimenter, building an elaborate barn for his stallions and a "pig palace" for his efforts in pig breeding. So it is fitting in the current vineyard emphasis on land use in Sonoma to explore a major agricultural experiment near Jack London Park. The winery doing revolutionary "organic" farming on a large commercial scale is the Benziger Family Winery at 1883 London Ranch Road, Glen Ellen; (707) 935–3000. The Benzigers provide an engaging tractor-trailer ride with narration through their property, showing their organic techniques of pest management and soil amendment. For example, predatory insect populations are enhanced to combat aphids. The organic debris from vine trimming is ground up and composted as a soil conditioner. After the tour you receive a complimentary glass of Benziger wine and can sample their more select "reserve" wines for a small fee.

Getting there

Drive north from the Bay Area on either Highway 101 or Freeway 880. Take the smaller Highways 116 or 121 until you reach the junction with Highway 12, then drive north on Highway 12 into Sonoma and beyond to Glen Ellen. Jack London State Historic Park is in Glen Ellen.

Writer Jack London's fabled Wolf House burned shortly after it was completed.

Be sure to see

Make your first stop the Jack London State Historic Park. In the town of Glen Ellen, be sure to stop in at the Jack London Bookstore, 14300 Arnold

Drive, 707-996-2888, which keeps alive the writer's legacy.

Best time to visit

Any time of the year is good. Spring is particularly inviting; the cool grass-lands display an abundance of wildflowers.

Lodging

The Gaige House Inn (13540 Arnold Drive, Glen Ellen, CA 95442; 800–935–0237; www.gaige.com) is a contemporary B&B for travelers who like stylish minimalist furniture rather than teddy bears. The owners, who deliberately chose the sleek furniture, preside over the hearty breakfasts and welcome visitors to an outdoor pool.

Dining

The Glen Ellen Inn (13670 Arnold Drive, Glen Ellen; 707–996–6409) epito-mizes a trend that the traveler benefits from throughout Northern California. Two young chefs, Karen and Christian Bertrand, who have both passion for food and the talent to create it, insisted on opening their own restaurant. Try their Fire and Ice Salad, followed by the lamb ravioli with sweet and spicy mustard.

For more information

Jack London State Historic Park is in Glen Ellen at 2400 London Ranch Road; (707) 938–5216, www.cal-parks.ca.gov.

The overall Sonoma tourism resource is the Sonoma County Tourism Program, 520 Mendocino Avenue #210, Santa Rosa, CA 95401; (800) 576–6662; www.sonomacounty.com.

23
Napa and Sonoma

The Father of Sonoma Agriculture: Luther Burbank's Legacy

Sonoma's boutique agriculture, supplying the great chefs of Northern California, owes much to "Plant Wizard" Luther Burbank, the most innovative horticulturist in California history. See where the magic began at Burbank's home in Santa Rosa and its adjacent gardens.

The historic story

The Luther Burbank Home and Gardens in Santa Rosa celebrates the pioneering work of this distinguished horticulturist, who started his work on a four-acre plot in Santa Rosa and expanded to another eighteen acres near Sebastopol.

Long before the dot-com companies of Silicon Valley made California world famous for electronics innovation, Luther Burbank was pioneering another critical area of the human endeavor. Burbank was developing the fruit, nut, and flower varieties that thrive especially in California. Partly because of his pioneering agricultural inventions, California produces nearly a third of the nation's food. Anyone with a delight in nature and gardening will enjoy touring the house, greenhouse, gardens, and museum.

Luther Burbank was born in Lancaster, Massachusetts, on March 7, 1849, and for more than fifty years made his home in Santa Rosa. In California his birthday is now celebrated as Arbor Day, and trees are planted in his memory.

One of Burbank's goals was to increase the world's food supply by altering the characteristics of plants. He developed a spineless cactus that could be grown in deserts and used as forage for livestock. In his long career Burbank bred more than 800 new varieties of plants, including more than 200 varieties of fruits, vegetables, nuts, and grains. He died in 1926 and was buried near his greenhouse on the property.

On a tour you see the gardens, home, greenhouse, and carriage house. The gardens cover more than an acre and have areas for medicinal herbs, cutting flowers, roses, wildlife habitats, and ornamental grasses. Many new horticultural introductions are displayed, giving both the common and botanic names for ease and accuracy of identification. The home is a Greek Revival house where Burbank lived beginning in 1884. His widow, Elizabeth, lived here until her death in 1977. The greenhouse was designed and built by Burbank in 1889 and includes a re-creation of his office with many of his garden tools. The carriage house has more exhibits about the ongoing impact of Burbank's life work.

Burbank's social circle included the other giants in their respective fields of innovation at the time. One famous photo shows him entertaining Henry Ford and Thomas Edison at his house.

He was an enthusiast about the Sonoma region for agriculture. "I firmly believe from what I have seen," he wrote in 1875, "that this is the chosen spot of all the earth as far as Nature is concerned."

The fitting complement to a look at Burbank's house is a ramble over rural Sonoma County using the Sonoma Farm Trails Map, readily available from any of the local tourism sources. With the map in hand, you can visit dozens of small producers who grow everything from apples to olallieberries. The map conveniently divides the county into areas. You can seek out who raises emus or shitake mushrooms. A calendar alerts you to the harvest periods, when you can buy harvested crops or even pick them yourself. Without the boutique farming of Sonoma, the celebrity chefs of Northern California would be stressed indeed.

Getting there

Santa Rosa is a main stop on Highway 101 going north from San Francisco. The Sonoma Farm Trails Map carries you to the far reaches of the region.

Be sure to see

The Luther Burbank Home and Gardens is at the corner of Santa Rosa and Sonoma avenues in Santa Rosa (707–524–5445; www.lutherburbank.org). The Farm Trails Map, available from the visitors bureau, can entice travelers to a day of wandering on the Sonoma back roads. Farm Trails also has its own Web site: www.farmtrails.org.

Apple blossoms line the Sonoma Farm Trails in spring.

Best time to visit

There is a year-round cycle of events that are especially good times to schedule a visit. On March 3, Burbank's birthday, there is the local Arbor Day festivity. From April 1 to October 1 the house is open for tours, led by docents every day except Monday. May features a Mother's Day Celebration of Victorian Handicrafts and a Luther Burbank Rose Parade Festival. For June's Garden Exposition, garden experts give demonstrations.

The gourmet produce fields of Sonoma County are lush for a long growing season, from late spring to autumn, so any time of the agricultural year can be interesting for the Farm Trails tours.

Lodging

For a small, family-owned lodging in Santa Rosa, a good choice is Hotel La Rose (308 Wilson Street, Santa Rosa, CA 95401; 707–579–3200; www.hotellarose.com). Hotel La Rose has anchored Santa Rosa's Old Railroad Square area since 1907.

Dining

John Ash & Company (4330 Barnes Road, Santa Rosa; 707–527–7687) is a highly regarded restaurant set in a forty-five-acre vineyard, emphasizing wine country regional cuisine under chef John Ash.

For more information

The overall Sonoma tourism resource is the Sonoma County Tourism Program, 520 Mendocino Avenue #210, Santa Rosa, CA 95401; (800) 576–6662; www.sonomacounty.com. For Santa Rosa tourist information contact the Santa Rosa Convention & Visitor Bureau, 9 Fourth Street, Santa Rosa, CA 95401; (800) 404–7673; www.visitsantarosa.com.

24

Napa and Sonoma

Quintessential Small Town America: Historic Healdsburg

With its nineteenth-century town plaza and its somewhat remote location, Healdsburg remains a satisfying glimpse of a quieter, rural-based California. Enjoy a progressive little town that hasn't been swept up in modernization.

The historic story

Harmon Heald founded a trading post and store at the site that was later named after him. It was he who laid out the town in a grid pattern, allowing for the central plaza that unifies the place.

When the railroad arrived in 1871, Healdsburg became a major produce and canning hub. The agricultural base of the region can still be enjoyed on drives around the region or at the farmers' market held on the plaza. The railroad also brought the first tourists here, who came to appreciate the Russian River, which flows through the area.

The classic Spanish-style plaza is the heart of the town. One block east of the plaza is the Healdsburg Museum, founded by William Langhart, which showcases exhibits on the pioneer and agricultural heritage. The museum has nineteenth-century clothing, firearms, and Pomo Indian baskets. Over 8,000 photos of the pioneer period are a special part of the collection. The museum building is a restored Carnegie Library, another little gem of Americana preserved.

Trees are a special pleasure of Healdsburg. You can get a *Tree Walk of Healdsburg* booklet from the Chamber of Commerce, guiding you to the many species planted in the plaza and in the surrounding streets. In the southwest corner of the plaza, where Center and Matheson Streets meet, there is a tree story that every explorer of California will enjoy. On one side of the walkway is a readily identifiable coast redwood, planted in the late 1800s. As many travelers know, the coast redwood also has an inland cousin, the giant redwoods of the Sierra foothills. However, the tree planted opposite the coast redwood is yet another long-lost cousin, the dawn redwood.

Botanists knew that the two California redwoods had a distant relative, found only in fossils. In one of the major botanical surprises of the twentieth century, in 1944, these "fossil" dawn redwoods were found to exist in a remote region of China. This dawn redwood on the Healdsburg plaza was planted here in 1953.

The Bradford pear trees planted along the west side of the plaza are a particularly effective street tree, with leaves brilliantly colored in the autumn. With the booklet in hand you can take a pleasant walk around town, viewing the specimen trees, which are wonderfully mature.

Historic homes of Healdsburg can be part of the same walk, so also pick up the historic homes flyer at the Chamber of Commerce. For example, the Adna Phelps House at 68 Front Street is an Italianate structure from 1875. It was built by Adna Phelps, a one-time carpenter who later became involved in local wineries. He sold to Peter and Giuseppe Simi, Italian immigrant brothers who founded the Simi winery.

Antiquing is a popular activity here. There are more than 20 antiques stores in the streets around the plaza. Three times a year, on Sundays close to Memorial Day, Fourth of July, and Labor Day, there is an outdoor antiques fair on the plaza. Many of the antiques shops are clustered together in collectives, such as Plaza Antiques (44 Mill Street). Fourteen shops can be seen at Healdsburg Classics (226 Healdsburg Avenue). Antique Harvest (225 Healdsburg Avenue) is one of the oldest shops and specializes in quality restorations.

Meandering through the rural-based agriculture, especially vineyard and winery complexes, is an interesting outing from Healdsburg. There are vineyards in all directions, more than sixty wineries and six different "appellations," or designated wine districts, to visit. The Dry Creek region to the northwest, Alexander Valley to the northeast, and Russian River to the southwest are the three main options. One pleasing trip would be a drive up the Dry Creek Valley to Lake Sonoma, with a few stops at wineries. Dry Creek Vineyard, 3770 Lambert Bridge Road, has picnic tables. At the end of the road is 2,700-acre Lake Sonoma, open to the public for fishing and picnicking. Maps with winery locations are readily available from the Chamber of Commerce.

Honor Mansion in Healdsburg is a fine example of a restored
Victorian turned into a beautiful B&B.

Getting there

Drive north from San Francisco 65 miles on Highway 101 until you see the Healdsburg turnoff, north of Santa Rosa. Turn east on Mill Street to reach the plaza.

Be sure to see

The plaza is worth some time. Sit on a bench, browse the shops and antique stores, or perhaps have lunch at the Charcuterie Restaurant on the edge of the plaza. Check out the Healdsburg Museum at 221 Matheson Street, walk the town to see the magnificent trees and early architecture (aided by booklets from the Chamber of Commerce), and conclude with an excursion into one of the adjacent wine regions, such as Dry Creek.

Best time to visit

Any time of the year is good for Healdsburg. For a small community it has an unusually large number of local festivals. The May Russian River Wine Festival/Antiques Fair or the June Jazz Festival would be congenial times for a visit.

Lodging

Honor Mansion (14891 Grove Street, Healdsburg, CA 95448; 800–554–4667; www.honormansion.com) is an example of the way B&B owners have restored Victorian structures and turned them into first-class lodgings. The proprietors have carefully nurtured the restoration of this 1883 Italianate home.

Dining

Healdsburg Charcuterie (335 Healdsburg Avenue; 707–431–7213) is a lunch spot adjacent to the plaza, with a cuisine they call "California Fresh" and an extensive local wine list. For a fine-dining evening, try Cafe Lolo (620 Fifth Street, Santa Rosa; 707–576–7822); the pan-roasted duck breast and the braised lamb shank are good choices.

For more information

Contact the Healdsburg Area Chamber of Commerce at 217 Healdsburg Avenue, Healdsburg, CA 95448; (707) 433–6935; www.healdsburg.org.

101   199

Crescent City •

Jedediah Smith
Redwoods
State Park

N

*Redwood
National Park*

*Del Norte Coast
Redwoods
State Park*

28   *Redwood
National Park*

*Prairie Creek
Redwoods
State Park*

• Orick

96

**Pacific
Ocean**

101

299

Eureka **27**

299

• Loleta
26 •Fernbridge
Ferndale

211   Scotia   36

101

*Humboldt
Redwoods
State Park*   **25**

Avenue of the Giants

Driving Tour ▬▬▬

0   10   20

MILES

Redwood Country

25

Redwood Country

Redwood Grandeur: Avenue of the Giants and the Company Town of Scotia

Consider all sides of the historic struggle to exploit and save California's redwoods as you drive along the awe-inspiring Avenue of the Giants and visit a town that lumber built.

The historic story

The historic and ongoing struggle to save redwood trees is one of the major stories in Northern California. Among the first substantial efforts to save redwoods in California was the creation of the Avenue of the Giants, a roadway adjacent to Highway 101 with many cathedral-like groves of trees. Avenue of the Giants begins 6 miles north of Garberville. Nearby, the main entity involved in cutting down the trees, Pacific Lumber, founded the company town of Scotia, whose mill and streets can be toured.

Redwoods flourish both north and south of San Francisco, but most of the groves worthy of the name Redwood Country are north. Redwoods grow in a narrow band of land proximate to the coast in a 400-mile strip from southern Oregon to Big Sur. About 3 percent of the original primeval forest of old-growth redwoods remains. Roughly half of that remaining forest is now in public hands and will never be cut.

The first reports of European contact with redwoods are in the diary of Crespi, a priest-botanist in the Portola expedition of 1769. The trees were unknown, of course, to Europeans. The first American to observe and comment on redwoods was intrepid explorer Jedediah Smith, who saw the trees in 1822. He is now honored in Redwood Country with a river and a state redwood park named after him.

Native Californians were well aware of the redwoods but did not consider their environment a hospitable habitat. Redwoods cast such shade that forage foods do not flourish under them. The bark does not burn well, and the redwood logs were too massive for Native Californians to cut into firewood. Yuroks along the north coast split redwood planks to build their shelters and hollowed out redwood logs for canoes.

Redwood trees (*Sequoia sempervirens*) are magnificent and are the tallest trees on earth (among the tallest examples are three trees at 367 feet in Redwood National Park, near Orick). The best introduction to these arboreal treasures is the important historic roadway of groves known appropriately as the Avenue of the Giants.

Redwood Country's main trees begin along Highway 101 north of Leggett at the Richardson Grove. A few miles farther north, you enter the 31-mile Avenue of the Giants. This extended landscape consists of seventy memorial groves and is part of 51,222-acre Humboldt Redwoods State Park.

Follow the side road at Phillipsville along Highway 101. Several turnoff areas invite you to pause and walk through the groves. Be sure to see all the groves on both sides of Highway 101 from Phillipsville to Redcrest.

Founder's Grove is one of the better stops, with trees about 2,500 years old. The Founder's Tree is 346.1 feet high and was formerly thought to be the highest. The Dyerville Giant—at 370 feet the tallest tree until it fell in 1991—can be seen in this grove. The fallen tree is 17 feet in diameter.

The drive along the Rockefeller Grove on Bull Creek Flats Road is a poignant example of the need to protect entire watersheds to save prize redwoods. Clear-cut slopes upstream from the prize Rockefeller trees exposed ground that washed into the creek in 1955 and 1964, subsequently undermining some of the giant trees. Silting of streams also damaged the salmon-spawning habitat. This peril would later instigate further protective measures to the north in Redwood National and State Parks.

The Humboldt Redwoods Interpretive Center (707–946–2263) at Burlington Campground is open year-round to dispense park information, maps, and books.

Besides the trees themselves, of course, there are the companies dedicated to cutting down the trees because consumers demand the product.

The company town of Scotia, the largest single mill for cutting redwoods, offers one of the most intriguing industrial tours in California. You can view the entire redwood cutting operation, starting with the power water jets that scrape off the bark and ending with the huge saws that select the best cuts of the wood. Scotia was built by the Pacific Lumber Company (707–764–2222) for its employees. Unfortunately, part of the town burned in a 1992 fire.

Scotia is an historic lumber mill town.

At a park in the center of Scotia you can see a cross section of a redwood tree 1,285 years old. The tree yielded 69,000 board feet of lumber. Children can scramble over an old logging locomotive on display at the park. Redwoods have a capacity to inspire wonder because of their height, beauty, and age. Even a tree seemingly 1,285 years old may, in fact, be countless eons older. Most redwoods sprout clonally from the roots of their parent tree rather than from seeds. This same tree may have perpetuated itself in this fashion for thousands upon thousands of years. There is a Scotia Museum to peruse at the corner of Main and Bridge Streets.

At shops throughout Redwood Country you can often see burls for sale. Burls are masses of tree tissue that form around a bud. They are attractive ornamentally and, if put in water, will sprout as a miniature tree. The shoots will grow for years, living off the nourishment stored in the burl.

Getting there

The famous redwoods are not difficult to locate. Simply head north from San Francisco along Highway 101. In about four hours you'll reach the first stately forests at small Richardson Grove. The first substantial groves are at Humboldt Redwoods State Park. Avenue of the Giants is just north of Humboldt. Scotia is on the west side of Highway 101.

Be sure to see

As you drive north stop at the visitor center in Humboldt Redwoods State Park to orient yourself. Once you reach in the Avenue of the Giants, many of the groves, such as the Founder's Grove, are truly impressive.

At Scotia be sure to tour the lumber operation and then spend some time enjoying the small town, where almost everything is made of redwood.

Best time to visit

Any time of year is good for exploring Redwood Country. Winters tend to be chilly and wet, the environment that makes redwood trees thrive. Summers can be foggy. Spring and autumn are ideal times of travel here. In whatever natural mood the trees are presented to you, they are inspiring.

Lodging

The Scotia Inn (100 Main Street, Scotia, CA 95565; 707–764–5683; www.scotiainn.com) is the historic place (opened 1888) to stay on this trip. The structure has twelve lodging rooms, rustic and economical.

Dining

The Scotia Inn's Redwood Dining Room offers both a regular menu and a monthly ethnic menu, which may be Southwestern or Greek. Try the goat cheese appetizer. Salmon or filet are specialties on the regular menu.

For more information

Humboldt Redwoods State Park has an informative Web site: www.humboldtredwoods.org.

A marketing organization representing all the tourism areas north of San Francisco, known as the Redwood Empire, is a useful resource for travelers. Their annual book on the region, the *Redwood Empire Adventures Travel Guide,* available for $3.00 postage and handling, covers all the counties. Contact the Redwood Empire Association at 2801 Leavenworth, Second Floor, San Francisco, CA 94133; (888) 678–8502; www.redwoodempire.com.

The most active tourism information source in the region is the Eureka/Humboldt County Convention and Visitors Bureau, 1034 Second Street, Eureka, CA 95501; (800) 346–3482; www.redwoodvisitor.org.

26

Redwood Country

Ferndale: The Victorian Village and Its Artists

Pockets of Victorian architecture flourished in various areas of Northern California, but nowhere else is it preserved in such a thorough and pleasant gingerbread manner as in Ferndale.

The historic story

The lumber and dairy industries that originally brought prosperity here have been augmented by tourism and art as engines of the local economy. Lumbering may be the more obvious story in Humboldt County, but the broad alluvial plain associated with the Eel River produced a second major resource—an abundance of grass that could sustain a huge dairy industry. Though Ferndale is 5 miles inland from the sea, its elevation is only 30 feet. While exploring the Eel delta, you can stop at the Loleta Cheese Company in the small village of Loleta. Sample some of their specialties, such as jalapeño-flavored jack cheese.

Ferndale is known for its Carpenter Gothic architectural legacy. Start with a look at one of the earliest structures, the Shaw House Inn (703 Main Street), aided by a handy foldout map in the souvenir edition of the Ferndale Enterprise, available free at most local shops. With map in hand, stroll down the 4 blocks of Main Street from Ocean to Shaw Streets. Aided by the map you will learn the nuances that distinguish the Eastlake-style Ferndale Meat Company (376 Main Street) from the Roman-style Ferndale Bank (394 Main).

As you might expect, several Victorian houses in addition to the Shaw House Inn have become B&Bs, including the Gingerbread Mansion Inn (400 Berding Street), Victorian Inn (400 Ocean Avenue), and Queen of Hearts (831 Main Street).

Hobart Brown and his art legacy represents another thread of the modern historical story. Brown arrived here in 1965 and started sculpting his metal creations. Be sure to visit his gallery at 393 Main Street. Brown also brought a zany sense of imagination. In 1969 he founded an annual event called the Kinetic Sculpture Race (707–786–9259), in which entrants must cover both water and land between Arcata and Ferndale in human-powered vehicles. For three days every Memorial Day weekend contestants scramble over a 36-mile course in contraptions of their own design.

The challenge of crossing water and land has spurred some ingenious creations. The race is a concourse of contraptions, and many entries from earlier years can be seen at a museum at 580 Main Street.

When Brown planned the first race, he was surprised to find that seven entrants and 10,000 spectators showed up. The race now attracts more than fifty entrants per year, including contestants from Japan to Canada, and has become a cult tourist attraction.

"We race for glory alone," says Brown. "The prize money for winning one year was a check for $6.75."

There are many other art galleries in Ferndale, featuring works by the about 100 artists who live among Ferndale's 1,240 residents.

The Ferndale Museum (corner of Shaw and Third Streets; 707–786–4466) contains many artifacts on the area history, especially the dairy industry that has flourished here since the town was founded in 1852.

Getting there

Drive north on Highway 101 and watch for the signs to Fernbridge/Ferndale, south of Eureka. Ferndale is a short drive west of Highway 101, across Fernbridge, an arched concrete span built in 1911.

Be sure to see

Walk around the historic town to see the Gingerbread Mansion and the Shaw House as examples of Victorian architecture.

Be sure to stop at the museum to the Kinetic Sculpture Race to view some of the wacko creations that characterize this annual event. Visit Hobart Brown's gallery and some of the other art galleries in town. Stop at the Ferndale Museum to absorb the region's dairy history. Then drive along the Eel River delta to enjoy the rural countryside, perhaps with a stop at the Loleta Cheese Factory (252 Loleta Drive, Loleta; 800–995–0453) for some picnic supplies, such as their smoked salmon cheddar.

The Gingerbread Mansion is an historic B&B in Ferndale.

Best time to visit

Memorial Day weekend's Kinetic Sculpture Race is a special time of year here. Call the Ferndale Chamber of Commerce to verify the actual dates. Beyond that, this lively little town has several other yearly festivals to consider: the Tour of the Unknown Coast bicycle race in May; the Scandinavian Festival and Parade in June; and the Humboldt County Fair and Horse Races in August. The Christmas Celebration includes "America's Tallest Living Christmas Tree" and a Lighted Tractor Parade.

Lodging

The Gingerbread Mansion (400 Berding Street, Ferndale, CA 95536; 800–952–4136; www.gingerbread-mansion.com) provides choice historic lodging. One block off Main Street, this restored Victorian has been filled with antiques by a couple who were smitten by the structure and the idea of relocating here in the early 1980s.

Dining

Curley's Grill (400 Ocean Avenue; 707–786–9696) in Ferndale epitomizes the fine dining without pretense that is characteristic of this friendly small town. Try the grilled tortilla and onion cake appetizer, perhaps followed by a Caesar salad or the roast pork loin in beer.

For more information

The local information source is the Ferndale Chamber of Commerce, P.O. Box 325, Ferndale, CA 95536; (707) 786–4477; www.victorianferndale. org/chamber.

The most active tourism information source in the region is the Eureka/Humboldt County Convention and Visitors Bureau, 1034 Second Street, Eureka, CA 95501; (800) 346–3482; www.redwoodvisitor.org.

27

Redwood Country

Eureka:
The Lumber Baron Town

Ship off to Eureka, port city for titans of timber like
William Carson, whose Victorian mansion is a landmark of
California architecture.

The historic story

Lumbering has been the main historical story associated with redwood country. Before roads were viable means of transport, the redwood lumber of far Northern California had to be shipped by boat to the ready markets of San Francisco. The wealth of the early lumber period expressed itself in Eureka, and when thinking of the lumber baron era, the place to stop and gaze is the William Carson Mansion. This lavish gingerbread Victorian, the finest nineteenth-century architectural legacy along the north coast, was built in 1884 at the corner of Second and M Streets.

William Carson became the timber tycoon of Eureka, but there were also many other prosperous folk. A brochure from the visitor bureau can alert you to a driving tour of Eureka with 125 structures from the Victorian era, highlighting styles ranging from Queen Anne to Carpenter Gothic.

Eureka's Clarke Memorial Museum has a permanent Victoriana display showing the parlor of a grand house. The museum also has many Native American artifacts, such as basketry, from the Hoopa, Karuk, and Yurok peoples.

The Humboldt Bay Maritime Museum (423 First Street; 707–444–9440) shows the rich maritime story of this largest bay and seaport in California north of San Francisco. Schooners carried the redwood from roughly seventy-five mills on Humboldt Bay to the San Francisco market at the height of lumbering.

Lumber baron William Carson's house was the most opulent
Victorian along the north coast.

The Virtues of Redwood

The tree's wood is soft and easy to saw. Though not as strong as Douglas fir, it has an attractive red color that can be stabilized to remain red or will weather naturally to a pleasing gray. It is widely used in house siding, decks, and garden lumber. The biggest virtue of redwood is its ability to withstand weathering and termites without deteriorating. Although prolonged moisture will cause most woods to rot, redwood will endure. Redwood is one of the most weather-resistant woods found in North America, competing with the cypress of the South.

Eureka's Old Town area, along Second and Third Streets from C to M Streets, has interesting shops. Blue Ox Mill Works (Foot of X Street; 707–444–3437) deals in the wood trimmings used to restore Victorians. They offer a tour of the mill and the Victorians that their skills enhance.

Fort Humboldt State Historic Park (707–445–6567), an 1850s military outpost at Eureka, has many exhibits about the early lumbering industry. One amazing tool of the trade was a huge winch, called a slackliner, used to bring large logs down steep slopes. Ulysses S. Grant was stationed at Fort Humboldt in 1853. He pursued his career as the victorious general in the Civil War and later became President of the United States.

The futures of both logging and fishing, the economic mainstays of the region, are uncertain, and the politics are equally intense. Depletion of the old-growth supply, rather than a diminishing demand, is a restricting factor in lumbering. However, redwood is the fastest-growing softwood species suited to this climate, and from a board-foot point of view, young forests are more productive than old forests. Fishing for salmon has been banned off parts of this coast in some years because the annual run of salmon in the Klamath River was perilously low. If you pass the mouth of the Klamath River when the salmon are spawning, you'll find a small army of RVs with salmon fishermen lined up reel-to-reel along the bank. Upstream on the Hoopa Native American reservation, residents are allowed to net the fish.

Getting there

Eureka is on Highway 101 north of the Avenue of the Giants and Ferndale. Allow six hours for the drive from San Francisco.

Be sure to see

The Carson Mansion, Second and M Streets, is a gem of California's

Victorian architecture. The house is now a private club and closed to the public, so enjoy it from the outside.

The Clarke Memorial Museum, at 240 E Street; (707) 443–1947, may have exhibits such as waterfowl hunting or Native American basketry.

In the Eureka Old Town area, have Jay Dottle of Hum Boats take you for a ride in his lovingly restored wooden boat, now a water taxi. His Hum-Boats is at the foot of F Street; (707) 443–5157.

Best time to visit

Any time of year is good for Eureka, but be aware of the seasonal pattern in Northern California. The long rainy winter, the fog of summer, and the glorious days of spring and autumn are all aspects of the annual weather pageant. A Dixieland Jazz Festival is held in March and a Blues on the Bay event in the last weekend in August. A large downtown hotel, the Eureka Inn, hosts a major Christmas celebration.

Lodging

Few other B&Bs in California have an historic completeness to equal Abigail's Elegant Victorian Mansion in Eureka (1406 C Street, Eureka, CA 95501; 707–444–3144; www.eureka-california.com). The building itself, one of the exceptional Victorian homes of the region, is an 1888 National Historic Landmark. The interior is filled with antiques and period mementos, including books, newspapers, and items from daily life of the Victorian era. The B&B is more of an interactive living-history house museum than a commercial lodging. The proprietors sometimes dress in period costumes and drive guests around in their vintage automobile.

Dining

The Hotel Carter's Restaurant 301 (301 L Street; 707–444–8062) is on the creative cutting edge of modern California cuisine. The restaurant has a garden-to-kitchen style based on its own gardens, which can be toured. Its wine list is a *Wine Spectator* Grand Award winner. Hotel Carter and Restaurant 301 are part of an intriguing historic complex known as the Carter House Inns. One building in the group is a re-creation of an 1884 San Francisco Victorian that was destroyed in the Earthquake and Fire of 1906.

For more information

The city and county tourism information source is the Eureka/Humboldt County Convention & Visitors Bureau, 1034 Second Street, Eureka, CA 95501, (800) 346–3482; www.redwoodvisitor.org.

28

Redwood Country

Redwood National and State Parks: Saving the Tallest Trees

The redwood forest exhibits a cathedral hush—so dense and dimly lit, so calm and eternal. You may find tears coming to your eyes as you commune with these monarchs of the mist.

The historic story

A more-recent phase in the historic saga of saving Northern California's redwoods involved setting aside whole watersheds. Unless the entire watershed could be protected from the silt of clear-cut slopes above it, the vulnerable shallow-rooted giants could easily be toppled.

Creating Redwood National and State Parks in 1968, preserving the tallest of the tall trees, was a milestone in California's awakening environmental awareness. The United Nations Educational, Scientific, and Cultural Organization (UNESCO) deemed Redwood National and State Parks a "world heritage site" in 1982, recognizing that redwoods are a phenomenon of worldwide interest. These arboreal giants have been flourishing for around twenty million years in a long, thin band along the coast from southwest Curry County in Oregon to south Monterey County in California, about 10 miles north of Hearst Castle.

One of the first Americans to observe redwoods was intrepid explorer Jedediah Smith, who saw the trees in 1822. He is now honored in Redwood Country with a river and a state park named after him.

Above Eureka, Highway 101 swings close to the coast and passes through major state redwood parks, such as Prairie Creek, Del Norte, and Jedediah Smith, located in the foggy and rainy environment so conducive to optimal redwood growth.

These state parks (some of which were set aside in the 1920s) and federal lands were combined in 1968 to become Redwood National and State Parks, an unusual shared-name designation. Prairie Creek Park is noted for its Fern Canyon and herds of Roosevelt elk. You may see as many as thirty wild elk at Prairie Creek, part of the 1,500-strong herd in the region. Del Norte Park contains attractive showings of rhododendrons and azaleas. Jedediah Smith Park, with its wild Smith River, is appreciated for its trout, salmon, and steelhead runs.

The interpretive center at Orick, the Redwood National and State Parks Information Center, is worth a stop to orient yourself. The center is perched right on the coast. Official headquarters for the parks is in Crescent City to the north.

One of the most enjoyable walks in the region is a loop in the Lady Bird Johnson Grove, which shows the range of vegetation, such as the twelve kinds of ferns, that grows in the redwood environment.

There are two ways to get close to some of the tallest trees, which are in Tall Trees Grove. This grove formerly contained the tallest redwood, but wind knocked off the top. The official tallest tree is now believed to be the Mendocino Tree (376 feet, 6 inches) in Montgomery Woods State Reserve near Ukiah. You can get a permit from the information center to drive within 1.3 miles of the grove and hike down (and back up) to view the tall trees. Alternatively, you can make a 15-mile and relatively level hike up and back Redwood Creek to see the trees. This hike is possible only in the dry season of summer and in autumn before the rains begin.

Along Highway 101 there are roadside attractions that screaming kids in the back of the car will never let you get past, such as the Tour Thru Tree at the Highway 169, Klamath Glen exit. Another attraction, Trees of Mystery, at first appears to be largely a tourist memento store, but be sure to see their End of the Trail Museum, with its elaborate Native American basketry and costume collection. Besides the Native American artifacts, such as a Crow elk tooth–adorned dress, you'll see a distinguished collection of Edward Curtis photos.

Quieter wonders, such as Patrick's Point State Park, 6 miles north of Trinidad, show part of the historic record. At Patrick's Point there is a re-created Yurok village with the structures that these north coast Indians lived in. Patrick's Point also boasts handsome stands of spruce and hemlock, plus some 350 varieties of mushrooms.

Getting there

Redwood National and State Parks are strung along Highway 101 north of

The Lady Bird Johnson Grove offers a pleasant walk in Redwood National Park.

Eureka. Various state parks are part of the national park, an unusual situation in park relationships.

Be sure to see

Stop first to orient yourself at the visitor center at Orick. If you are equal to the hike, walk in to see some of the tall trees. For an easier and engaging walk in the redwood environment, meander along the Lady Bird Johnson Trail.

Best time to visit

Unless you are a storm-watching enthusiast who likes to celebrate the winter rainstorms, other times of the year will be more congenial in Redwood National and State Parks. Late spring and autumn can be a delight, as can summer, though summer mornings can sometimes be foggy.

Lodging

Southport Landing (444 Phelan Road, Loleta, CA 95551; 707–733–5915) is a fitting historic B&B for the theme of this trip. It remains an historic structure in a bucolic and rustic rural setting on the south side of Humboldt Bay. In the 1890s, the area was a busy shipping point for potatoes, salmon, and lumber from the Eel River delta. From the house you can kayak (with Southport's kayaks), hike around the wildlife refuge on the bay, and bike (with their bikes) out to the ocean or to the nearby town of Loleta.

Dining

In Redwood National and State Parks, though you are out in the woods, gourmet dining is available at Rolf Rheinschmidt's place, Rolf's Park Cafe (707–488–3841), at the Fern Canyon exit off Highway 101. Try the smoked salmon or the restaurant specialty, a combo plate of buffalo, elk, and boar.

For more information

You can request a brochure from the Superintendent, Redwood National Park, 1111 Second Street, Crescent City, CA 95531; (707) 464–6101. Each national park has its own informative page on the Park Service Web site. The url for this park is www.nps.gov/redw. Peruse this site before visiting.

The park visitor center is clearly marked as an exit point in Orick, north of Eureka.

The regional tourism information source is the Eureka/Humboldt County Convention & Visitors Bureau, 1034 Second Street, Eureka, CA 95501; (800) 346–3482; www.redwoodvisitor.org.

96

5

139

3

97

MILES
0   10   20

Mount Shasta

Dunsmuir   McCloud   89

3

5

299

Trinity Center

Weaverville Joss House
State Historic Park

Shasta
Lake

299

89

Weaverville   Shasta
Dam

299   30

Shasta   Redding

44   Lassen
Volcanic
National
Park

89

89

273

Lassen Peak
10,457 feet   29

44   Drakesbad

36

5   36

36

Red Bluff

32

N

99

32

70

Shasta-Cascade Region

29

Shasta-Cascade Region

Apocalypse in California: When Lassen Peak Erupted

The unexpected and explosive eruption of Lassen Peak caught the imagination of the entire United States. Discover why those close to the volcano thought the Day of Judgment had arrived.

The historic story

Volcanoes and glaciers are the main players in the geologic history of Northern California. From Napa's Mt. St. Helena all the way north to Mt. Rainier near Seattle, the volcanic mountains have periodically erupted, shaping the landscape.

Within the memory of the non–Native Americans in California, the explosions of Lassen Peak were the main nonearthquake geologic events. On May 30, 1914, the "extinct" plug volcano displayed the first of over 180 steam explosions. On May 19, 1915, a river of lava poured a thousand feet down the mountain, creating a mudflow a .25-mile wide and 18 miles long. Three days later, a dramatic event called the Great Hot Blast shot debris 5 miles into the air and felled pine trees like bowling pins around the base of the mountain. During one eruption, inches of ash fell as far away as Reno.

The Loomis Museum, near the northwest entrance of Lassen Volcanic National Park, houses a dramatic display of historic photos of the catastrophe.

A drive on the Loop Road through Lassen Volcanic National Park acquaints you with the full range of this geologic drama. The Loop Road entrances to the park are near the southwest and northwest corners.

Two other park entrances are interesting, but they require substantial drives; consult maps carefully. An entrance at the northeast corner takes you

Fire and Ice

To understand how California was formed, two major geological realities need to be understood.

In the northern region volcanoes were the creators. Periodic eruptions of Lassen and Shasta redesigned the landscape and spread ash over wide areas.

Further south glacial ice was the carver, cutting through the granite of the mountains. Glacial force can be appreciated especially in Yosemite Valley, where you can look up at the scraped granite sides of Half Dome and El Capitan.

to a geologically textbook-perfect cinder cone, for which Lassen is famous. The southeast corner entrance takes you to some lovely lakes, such as Juniper Lake, and to the historic lodging known as Drakesbad.

Before the arrival of Europeans, Lassen was populated in summer by Atsugewi, Yana, Yahi, and Maidu peoples. The men hunted deer and the women gathered acorns and basket-weaving materials. In 1911 a Yahi Indian named Ishi appeared in nearby Oroville. He had never met whites before, and his tribe was thought to be extinct. He lived out his remaining days at the University of California, Berkeley, befriended by two anthropologists.

To learn more about the early inhabitants of Lassen, read the poignant book, *Ishi in Two Worlds* by Theodora Kroeber.

Getting there

Drive north on Interstate 5; turn east at Red Bluff on Highway 36, then north on Highway 89 to reach the southwest entrance to the park near the town of Mineral.

Be sure to see

The best way to see Lassen is to enter at the southwest corner, beyond Mineral, and drive the Loop Road, the main road through the park. The park's *Road Guide* will alert you to all the important stops.

Allow time for stops, such as the relatively level three-hour, 3-mile hike to the thermal area called Bumpass Hell. Bumpass is a choice walk amidst sulfurous fumaroles and other bubbling and hissing reminders of the live geologic energy below. Another hike, more invigorating, could take you to the

The Chaos Jumbles area in Lassen Volcanic National Park tells the story of past volcanic eruptions.

top of Lassen Peak. Lassen Peak's summit is at 10,457 feet, so be careful not to overexert yourself in the high altitude.

On the way out, stop at the Loomis Museum at the northwest corner to view the historic photos.

Best time to visit

Lassen is locked up with snow and ice for winter and well into spring, although it's accessible to the snowshoe enthusiast and cross-country skier. By June the park begins to open up and is a joy all summer and through the autumn until the first snows make driving the Loop Road treacherous. In an era when many other national parks are crowded in summer, Lassen remains relatively undiscovered, getting only about 400,000 visitors per year.

Lodging

The historic lodging of note here is Drakesbad Guest Ranch (Warner Valley Road, Chester, CA 96020; 530–529–1512), accessible at the southeast corner of the park. E. R. Drake founded a ranch here over a hundred years ago.

Drakesbad is comfortable but rustic, offering a full-service lodging plan that includes all meals. Drakesbad also organizes horse-packing trips into Lassen, which allows you to see more of the terrain in a short time than you could on foot. For a B&B with a stunning view of the upper Sacramento Valley from an elevated position, try Weston House (P.O. Box 276, Shingletown, CA 96088; 530–474–3738; www.westonhouse.com).

Dining

Fine dining is available at Drakesbad for patrons of the resort. Basic fast-food service is available at the southwest and northwest entrances to the park. If you're on a day trip, consider returning to Redding for dinner at C. R. Gibbs (2300 Hilltop Avenue; 530–221–2335) or Pio Loco (1135 Pine Street; 530–246–2111), where the salmon dressing is a specialty.

For more information

Request a brochure from the Superintendent, Lassen Volcanic National Park, P.O. Box 100, Mineral, CA 96063-0100; (530) 595–4444. The park boasts an unusually good range of publications on the history, flora, and fauna of the park. Books and maps can be ordered from the Loomis Museum Association (530–595–3399) to help you better enjoy the park. See also the National Park Service Web site for Lassen at www.nps.gov/lavo.

A main tourism information source for the region is the Redding Convention & Visitors Association, 777 Auditorium Drive, Redding, CA 96001; (800) 874–7562; www.ci.redding.ca.us.

30

Shasta-Cascade Region

Shasta City and Dam: The Northern Gold Rush and the Enduring Wealth of Water

Despite historic gold strikes, the enduring wealth of California lies in its agriculture. Tour a fascinating area touched by precious metal and home to an even more-precious resource—water.

The historic story

Though the great burst of the Gold Rush occurred in the foothills east of Sacramento, one intriguing more northerly strike happened west of the present-day city of Redding. Pierson B. Reading discovered gold along Clear Creek in 1848, setting off a rush centered on the small town of Shasta, now a state historic park.

But true wealth in California was not primarily to be found in precious metal. The enduring wealth was in agriculture if a stable water supply could be assured. The building of Shasta Dam (1938–1945) could be said to be the defining economic event of the twentieth century in Northern California.

The historic story begins with the various Native American groups, the Wintu, Yana, Chomawi, and Atsugewi peoples. They lived confortably, nurtured by the legendary runs of salmon in the rivers, the acorns to be harvested on the hillsides, and the abundance of deer and elk in the grasslands.

In the 1820s mountain men like Jedediah Smith and Peter Skene Ogden led fur trappers into the region.

As you approach the region the town of Red Bluff has two interesting historic houses to visit. William B. Ide Adobe State Historic Park (3040 Adobe Road; 530–529–8599) interprets the pioneer and later Victorian era in the region, with rangers in period costume. Ide had been president of the aborted California Republic, a brief political hiccup of 1846 (see chapter 21). The Kelly/Griggs House Museum (311 Washington Street; 530–527–1129) is a Victorian showplace built in the 1880s by sheepman Sidney Allen Griggs and purchased by the Kelly family in the 1930s. Garbed mannequins "live" among the antique furnishings and paintings. One room is devoted to Ishi, the last of the Yahi Indians (see chapter 29).

Once you reach Redding and Shasta Lake, a tour of Shasta Dam and possible water recreation, especially houseboating, is enticing. The building of Shasta Dam tamed three major rivers—the Pit, McCloud, and Sacramento—creating California's largest man-made reservoir. The dam reduced flooding, provided assured water for agriculture, and created 370 miles of wooded shoreline for recreation. Shasta Dam is the second largest concrete structure in the United States (after Grand Coullee on the Columbia River).

Free tours of the dam are informative and interesting. To arrange a tour contact the visitor center at 16349 Shasta Dam Boulevard, Shasta Lake; (530) 275–4463. There are a dozen competent providers of houseboats for recreational use around the lake.

Beyond the lake, the drive west from Redding on Highway 299 and then north on Highway 3 presents one of the most scenic and historic backcountry trips possible in Northern California.

First stop on this drive is Shasta City. The redbrick facades of Shasta State Historic Park can be perused as you absorb the huge prosperity that a gold strike can bring to a remote region. Shasta City and the town of Jacksonville, near Ashland, Oregon, were the prominent northern gold discovery sites. Shasta was the "Queen City" of the northern mines in the 1850s. Be sure to see the museum in the courthouse (530–243–8194), with its strong collections of California landscape art and Pit River Indian basketry. Across the street, the Litch General Store has been restored to its original condition.

Beyond Shasta City on Highway 299 is Weaverville and Weaverville Joss House State Historic Park (530–623–5284). There were 2,500 Chinese men seeking gold along the Trinity River in 1852. The Joss House was their place of Taoist worship. The life of the Chinese was tragically difficult in early California. They were not allowed to form families or bring their women and children from China, and they were discriminated against when they became prosperous.

Driving north on Highway 3, you'll experience some fascinating backcountry ranches, gold dredges along the rivers, stage stops from the horse-

Shasta State Historic Park was the scene of the northern Gold Rush.

stage era, and small museums. The Fort Jones Museum (11913 Main Street, Fort Jones; 530–468–5568) houses an elaborate Native American collection of basketry, ceremonial rocks, mortars, and pestles. The Scott Museum in Trinity Center (100 Airport Road, Trinity Center; 530–266–3378) exhibits many pioneer artifacts saved by native son Edwin Scott.

At some point in this circular trip you will pass through Redding, which has the most developed traveler services in the area. Redding also boasts an interesting interpretive site, where the wise use of the 375-mile Sacramento River is the theme. Be sure to stop by the Turtle Bay Park and Museum (800 Auditorium Drive; 800–887–8532) to absorb this modern vision of sustainable stewardship of the river.

Getting there

The Highway 5 corridor north from the Bay Area is the access route. At Redding side roads Highway 299 and Highway 3 to the west complete the route.

Be sure to see

The two historic houses of Red Bluff will acquaint you with the pioneer period. A tour of Shasta Dam tells the tale of the economic powerhouse of modern California agriculture. Then the drive west and north, Highways 29 and 3, takes you to the historic small towns, including Shasta City, Weaverville, and Fort Jones. Finally, the Turtle Bay Museum in Redding presents a future-looking vision for managing the resources of the great Sacramento River.

Best time to visit

This is a particularly good summertime drive. The weather is sunny and warm, and the elevation keeps it from becoming too hot. Expect rain and snow in winter. Redding has the liveliest festivals in the region, including Kool April Nites and the Shasta Jazz Festival, both in April. Red Bluff hosts one of the West's biggest rodeos each April.

Lodging

Vintage railroad cabooses have been gathered in Dunsmuir to create a one-of-a-kind lodging known as Railroad Park Resort (100 Railroad Park Road, Dunsmuir, CA 96025; 800–974–7245). Fans of rail Americana will enjoy this lodging opportunity.

Dining

A restaurant in two historic rail dining cars is another part of the tour de force known as Railroad Park, suggested above for lodging. Cafe Maddalena (5801 Sacramento Avenue, Dunsmuir; 530–235–2725) gets high praise from the locals as "the best restaurant north of Sacramento."

For more information

The main tourism information source for the region is the Redding Convention & Visitors Bureau, 777 Auditorium Drive, Redding, CA 96001; (800) 874–7562; www.ci.redding.ca.us. All the state historic parks have Web pages at www.cal-parks.ca.gov.

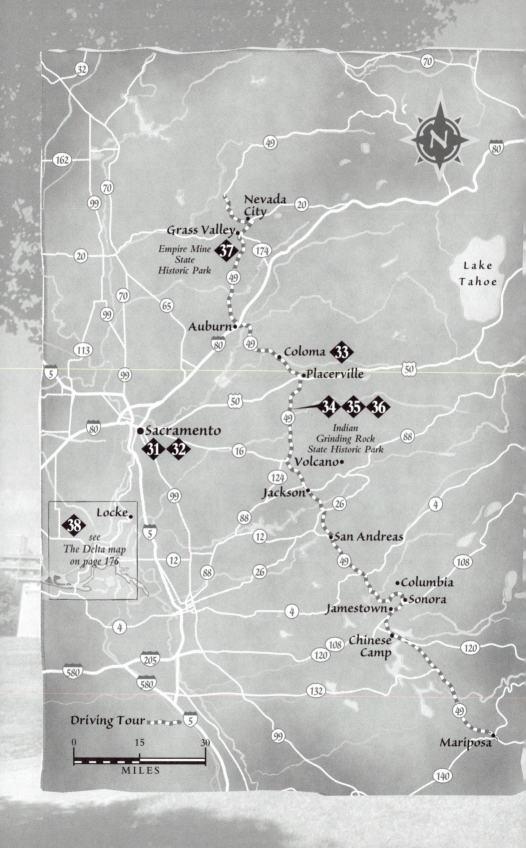

32

70

162

70

99

20

49

Nevada
City

20

80

Grass Valley

Empire Mine
State
Historic Park

37

174

Lake
Tahoe

80

49

65

20

70

99

Auburn

80

49

113

5

99

50

Coloma

33

Placerville

50

80

50

49

34 35 36

Sacramento

Indian
Grinding Rock
State Historic Park

88

31 32

16

Volcano

124

Jackson

99

88

12

26

88

12

Locke

38

see
The Delta map
on page 176

5

San Andreas

4

108

49

Columbia

120

Sonora

Jamestown

4

26

4

Chinese
Camp

108

120

120

205

580

132

99

49

580

Driving Tour

5

Mariposa

0   15   30

140

MILES

Sacramento and the Gold Country

31

Sacramento and the Gold Country

Dreams of an Agricultural Empire: John Sutter's Visions

Before the gold rush, there was John Sutter's vision. Visit Sutter's Fort, and imagine what California might have been if gold had never been discovered.

The historic story

Sacramento and the surrounding Delta have been the land of visionaries.

First came John Sutter, the Swiss entrepreneur, who carved out a trading and agriculture settlement at the confluence of the Sacramento and American Rivers in 1839.

In 1848 James Marshall, a sawmill worker for Sutter, discovered traces of gold in a millrace 30 miles to the east. In the years that followed, hundreds of thousands of adventurers from around the globe converged on Sacramento. They paid their way to San Francisco or arrived as deckhands and jumped ship in San Francisco harbor. Taking a steamer, they passed through the Delta and on to Sacramento, where they provisioned for the trip to the mines.

The Delta has some of the richest farmlands in the world. Those with a steadier vision saw that when you could sell eggs or apples for a dollar apiece, fortunes were to be made in the provisions. One of these visionaries was a Sacramento hardware store owner named Leland Stanford, who would later become railroad builder, governor, and university founder.

Before the arrival of John Sutter, California Native Americans flourished here in great numbers. They lived off the herds of tule elk and deer, the migrating ducks, and the salmon. Where the land pushed higher than the marshes, there were thousands of valley oak and black oak trees, whose acorns supplied half the Indian diet. Today you can see many Indian artifacts in the

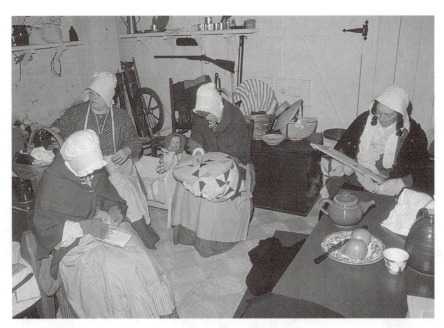

At Sutter's Fort you can see re-enactments of typical pioneer-era activities.

California State Indian Museum (2618 K Street; 916–324–0971) near Sutter's Fort. Hunting and fishing gear, basketry, dance regalia, musical instruments, and a hand-carved canoe are on display.

Sutter's proper name was Johann Augustus. He had received a 48,000-acre land grant from Mexican Governor Alvarado, who was then in charge of California. Sutter named his whitewashed fort New Helvetia after the Latin for his native Switzerland. You can visit the reconstructed fort at 2701 L Street (916–445–4422). Exhibits include the workplaces of carpenters, coopers, and blacksmiths; the fort prison; and living quarters of the frontier period.

It is worth noting that Sacramento's early history is not a story of Spanish-Mexican settlements, as is the rest of California to the south. San Francisco and Sonoma were as far north as the Spanish colonial thrust of missions, forts, and settlers reached. In the early 1800s it looked as though the northern part of present-day California might fly the flag of Russia or England, rather than Spain/Mexico.

The decisive event in the history of the area was, of course, the discovery of gold at Sutter's Mill by James Marshall in 1848. When miners overran his agricultural lands and destroyed his property, Sutter never fully recovered; he died an impoverished and unappreciated man.

Downtown Sacramento

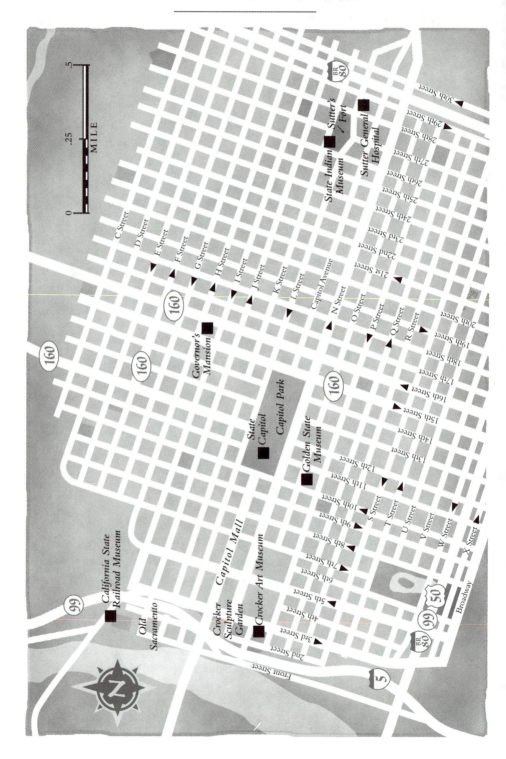

Before the Gold Rush, Sutter set a grand pattern of hospitality and initiative for the first settlers who came across the Sierras in wagons to California in 1841. It's poignant to visit Sutter's Fort and imagine what California might have been like if gold had never been discovered.

Getting there

In the nineteenth century you would have journeyed here by boat, taking a steam paddle wheeler from San Francisco through the Delta and up the Sacramento River to Sacramento, gateway to the gold mines.

As the true gold of agriculture became the obvious regional treasure, efforts were made to join Sacramento with the East by means of a railroad across the Sierra Nevada.

Today speedy Interstate 80 joins San Francisco and Sacramento, 90 miles to the northeast. Enthusiasts for the nostalgia of an earlier era will take a more leisurely route between San Francisco and Sacramento. Highway 160 from the East Bay snakes along the levees of the Sacramento River, passing small towns such as Walnut Grove and the agricultural abundance of pear orchards and asparagus.

Be sure to see

Sutter's Fort is at 2701 L Street in Sacramento. The California State Indian Museum is just around the corner at 2618 K Street.

Best time to visit

Any time is good, but times of re-enactment at Sutter's Fort are particularly enchanting. Each March there is a major Sutter's Fort Living History day. (Call for exact date; the festivities are repeated as the year proceeds.) Locals play the historic characters, including Sutter and Marshall, and re-create some of the skills of the day, such as cooking over an open fire and sewing clothes.

Lodging

Three elegant historic mansions form the fourteen-room Amber House Bed & Breakfast Inn (1315 Twenty-second Street, Sacramento, CA 95816; 800–755–6526; www.amberhouse.com).

Dining

Old Sacramento, not far from Sutter's Fort, has several good restaurants. One is The Firehouse (1112 Second Street; 916–442–4772), a brick building that was one of the first restorations in the area. Try the Sutter Devil Bones, beef bones with plenty of meat on them, or Hangtown Fries, an oyster-and-egg omelet that was a Gold Rush legend.

For more information

Contact the Sacramento Convention and Visitors Bureau, 1303 J Street, Suite 600, Sacramento, CA 95814; 916–264–7777; www.sacramentocvb.org. Sutter's Fort is at Twenty-seventh and L Streets (916–445–4422) and has a state park Web site at www.cal-parks.ca.gov.

Sacramento and the Gold Country

The Iron Road Across the Sierra: Old Sacramento and the Railroad Museum

The development of the American West rode in on the rails. Next stop: the California State Railroad Museum. Hear the story where the dream began.

The historic story

Within Sacramento, besides Sutter's Fort and the Indian Museum, your main stop should be Old Sacramento, with brief additional visits to the State Capitol, the Crocker Art Museum, the Governor's Mansion, and the Golden State Museum.

The dream of a transcontinental railroad began in Old Sacramento. An engineer named Theodore Judah made the proposal, but as the scheme developed he lost control to the so-called Big Four, a group of prosperous Sacramento merchants. Construction of the mammoth project began in 1863; in 1869 at Promontory, Utah, the western rails joined the Union Pacific pushing forth from the East.

Old Sacramento re-creates and preserves the Gold Rush and railroad era from 1850 to 1890. The California State Railroad Museum is one of the finest rail museums in the country, interpreting the many impacts railroads had on the lifestyle of the West. Old Sacramento includes an historic riverfront area and a twenty-eight-acre national historic landmark. The Gold Rush miners passed through this embarcadero, overrunning Captain John Sutter's nascent agricultural community in 1848.

Begin an historic tour at the B. F. Hastings Building at Second and J

The Big Four Building in Old Sacramento commemorates the four merchants who collaborated to build the Central Pacific Railroad.

Streets. The structure was once the first western office of the Pony Express and the home of the California Supreme Court from 1855 to 1869. Now there is a Wells Fargo Museum on the property.

While exploring here, seek out the forlorn bust of Theodore Judah at Second and L streets. It was Judah, the engineer, who had the original dream of the railroad and who persuaded the Big Four to build it. Judah, however, was squeezed out in the political struggle over control of the railroad.

Also rendered irrelevant by changing technology was the Pony Express, whose riders are memorialized in Old Sacramento with a bronze statue of a galloping horse and rider at the corner of Second and J Streets. Sacramento was the western terminus of the Pony Express, which ran 1,966 miles from St. Joseph, Missouri, to Sacramento in 1860. Using eighty riders the Pony Express could carry a letter over the route in ten days. By 1861, however, the transcontinental telegraph put the Pony Express out of business.

At 113 I Street lies the Big Four Building, where the four merchants— Leland Stanford, C. P. Huntington, Charles Crocker, and Mark Hopkins— drew up plans to build the Central Pacific Railroad. The Big Four Building now serves as part of the facade for the California State Railroad Museum (125 I Street; 916–445–6645). The museum re-creates a Central Pacific passenger station built in 1867, the first California station for the transcontinental railroad. The extensive museum holdings include twenty-one restored locomotives and cars, forty-six more one-of-a-kind exhibits, including re-created railroad waiting rooms and offices, plus films and photographs.

The reconstructed Eagle Theatre (925 Front Street), which opened in 1849, was California's first theater building.

After you leave Old Sacramento, stop by the domed State Capitol Building (Eleventh and L Streets; 916–324–0333), from 1874. Guided tours are available. Museum rooms in the capitol recall California's governors and politics through the years.

A further interesting stop is the Crocker Art Museum (216 O Street; 916–264–5423). The Crocker is the oldest art museum in the west. It was built by Judge Edwin B. Crocker in 1873 to house his private art collection. The museum shows nineteenth- and twentieth-century California art, some Old Masters, and various Asian pieces.

An 1877 Victorian that was the Governor's Mansion is now a museum (Sixteenth and H Streets; 916–323–3047). Thirteen of California's governors from 1913 to 1967 lived in the structure.

The newest history museum in Sacramento is the Golden State Museum (1020 O Street; 916–653–7524), which tells the ongoing story of California through its "Place, People, Promise and Politics." This museum strives to portray what is singularly Californian—from a nineteenth-century San Quentin "mug" book to paraphernalia from many political campaigns.

Getting there

Sacramento is 90 miles (about an hour and a half) east of San Francisco on Interstate 80. As you approach Sacramento look for the OLD SACRAMENTO turnoff sign. The road takes you across the Sacramento River; Old Sacramento is on your immediate left.

Be sure to see

The California State Railroad Museum is the highlight of Old Sacramento. The immense dome of the California State Capitol suggests the power of California. The three other suggested Sacramento museums can make your visit a full and exciting day.

Best time to visit

Any time of year is good for Old Sacramento. The Sacramento Jazz Jubilee in late May, billed as the largest traditional jazz festival in the world with more than one hundred bands, is an especially festive affair.

Lodging

The Delta King Hotel (1000 Front Street, Sacramento, CA 95814; 916–444–5464; www.deltaking.com) along the Old Sacramento waterfront is the historic inn for the region. The *Delta King* was once an actual riverboat plying the waters between San Francisco and Sacramento. It has now been modernized to function as a permanent hotel.

Dining

Rio City Cafe (1110 Front Street; 916–442–8226) is a lively restaurant along the Sacramento waterfront, offering a venue in the open air for enjoying the river and the scene. Try the grilled salmon.

For more information

Contact the Sacramento Convention and Visitors Bureau at 1303 J Street, Suite 600, Sacramento, CA 95814; (916) 264–7777; www.sacramentocvb.org. Old Sacramento has its own Web site: www.oldsacramento.com. All the museums in this museum-rich city can be accessed at www.sacmuseums.org.

33

Sacramento and the Gold Country

One Lucky Day at the Sawmill: How James Marshall Discovered Gold at Coloma

All that glitters may not be gold—but it was for James Marshall that fateful day in 1848. Dig into the history of the gold rush at Coloma's Gold Discovery site.

The historic story

In 1848 James Marshall was building a sawmill at Coloma on the American River for himself and his partner, Sacramento entrepreneur John Sutter. One day he noticed a couple of shiny flecks caught in the millrace. Marshall Gold Discovery State Historic Park celebrates how the Gold Rush began. The famous logging chute has been re-created at the site. It was from here that Marshall came running back to his workers with the news on January 24, 1848, "Boys, I believe I've found a gold mine."

Marshall waited several days before returning to Sutter's Fort to tell Sutter. Both Sutter and Marshall made extensive assay tests on the metal and sought to suppress the news once they learned the truth, but the story of gold was too enthralling to keep secret. San Francisco had 460 people at the time; Sacramento, 150. It was enterprising merchant Sam Brannan who paraded the news in San Francisco that there had been a gold strike on the American River.

With the rush of miners, wealth eluded Marshall, who died an impoverished and disappointed man, but others were luckier. Near Columbia, for example, someone had the good fortune to find a solid gold nugget that weighed 195 pounds. The search for the Mother Lode, that vein of pure gold, was on.

At Marshall Gold Discovery State Historic Park you can see artifacts from the gold-mining era, including this stamp mill.

What is impressive about Marshall Gold Discovery State Historic Park is that the large acreage preserves the entire town area. Most of the buildings are now mere memories, but a few remain, such as the Robert Bell Store. The Coloma Schoolhouse, a white wood structure, shows what a thriving waterfront community once existed here. The visitor center has a museum with examples of large gold nuggets, such as miners dreamed of, and an unrestored Concord stagecoach, the plushest of the bone-jarring devices that brought some folks overland to California.

Other gold-mining paraphernalia on display include stamp mills used to pulverize rock into more manageable sizes from which the grains of gold could be extracted. Recreational gold panning occurs across the river, north of the bridge. On a hill above the site is a statue of James Marshall pointing down to where he discovered gold. Hikers enjoy the Monroe Ridge Trail leading away from the statue site. From high points on the ridge you get a panoramic view of the valley.

The Gold Rush transformed the area within a few months. By the summer of 1848 a thousand miners were sifting gravel from the stream. The monumental discovery of precious metal in California in 1848 provoked one of the most frenzied voluntary migrations in human history and quickly settled what would become a major geographic and cultural entity, California.

Other locations in the Gold Country carry the story forward. Columbia State Historic Park re-creates the brief, democratic period when the common man, if lucky, could get rich by panning for nuggets in chilly mountain streams. Empire Mine State Historic Park is a memorial to the later period in gold extraction, when highly capitalized companies mined the quartz rock deep underground in search of veins of gold. Malakoff Diggins is a tragic testament to how man can, and will, destroy the environment in the name of greed.

The Gold Country still conjures up the excitement that James Marshall felt when he first noticed the gold nuggets. Gold Rush Country functions as a massive outdoor living museum, 300 miles long and about 20 miles wide if you begin at Mariposa in the south and drive north beyond Sierraville.

Today you can bathe in the nostalgic memories of the wild mining era while gazing at the many preserved buildings from the Gold Rush period. You can lodge in old Gold Rush–era hotels and Victorian houses, now B&Bs. You can visit the intriguing museums, poke about the small towns, and, if you are ambitious, even pan for flakes of your own.

Getting there

The most direct route to Coloma is Interstate 80 east to Sacramento, then

Highway 50 east to Highway 49. Turn north on Highway 49 to reach Coloma.

Getting there is easier today than it was for the miners, who had three alternatives. From the eastern United States they could sail 15,000 miles around Cape Horn. Panama offered a shorter but hotter and malaria-ridden crossing. The prospective miner could also push overland on wagon train trails, but these were as yet poorly marked. Weather and Indians were equally hostile. The bravado of the mining era can be read in the motto, "The cowards never started, and the weaklings died on the way."

Be sure to see

Marshall Gold Discovery State Historic Park is at Coloma on Highway 49.

Best time to visit

Coloma is a good place to visit any time of year. Each January 24 there is a special Gold Discovery Day festival. In June a Coloma Fest includes costumed reenactors. Coloma also hosts a 49er Family Festival in October with further emphasis on living-history demonstrations.

Lodging

In Coloma itself, a B&B steeped in history is the 1852 Coloma Country Inn (345 High Street, Coloma, CA 95613; 530–622–6919; www. colomacountryinn.com). Because fire was such a scourge among the wooden buildings of the Gold Rush period, an inn from 1852, only four years after the discovery of gold, is a treasure to be appreciated.

Dining

Italian restaurants are popular in the Gold Country. In the later part of the Gold Rush many Italian families came to the area as vegetable and grape farmers. Nine miles south of Coloma in Placerville, a good choice is Mama de Carlo's (482 Main Street; 530–626–1612).

For more information

All the state parks of California have individual Web sites at www.cal-parks.ca.gov. Contact Marshall Gold Discovery State Historic Park at 310 Back Street, Coloma, CA 95613; (530) 622–3470.

34

Sacramento and the Gold Country

Rambling Historic Highway 49: Starting with Columbia, the Preserved Gold Rush Town

The gold vein ran all through the foothills—from Mariposa in the south to beyond Grass Valley in the north—roughly along today's Highway 49. Follow the search for precious metal as you ramble along the highway and explore a preserved mining town.

The historic story

Columbia State Historic Park, just north of Sonora off Highway 49, amounts to an entire Gold Rush town preserved and restored. There you can actually pan for gold today at the Matelot Mining Co. and receive a demonstration of how it was done. You can peer in through the iron shutters of the Wells Fargo Express Building and ride one of the stages that carried a half billion dollars in gold dust (at today's prices) back to San Francisco between 1850 and 1870. Along your route the legendary robber Black Bart may relieve the stage of its fortune.

On March 27, 1850, Dr. Thaddeus Hildreth and his brother, George, made camp here and discovered gold. Within a month several thousand miners converged on the site, then known as Hildreth's Diggings, later Columbia.

While strolling about Columbia, you get a sense of what life was like for the 15,000 miners who lived here at the peak of mining. A museum in the brick Knapp Building exhibits the different mining techniques. At the Old Franco cabin you'll see what a typical miner's domestic life was like. A walk through town will take you by a Mexican fandango dancing hall, a blacksmith shop, and the 1861 schoolhouse.

Black Bart

Black Bart, aka respectable San Francisco citizen Charles E. Bolton, became a Robin Hood folk figure in California and his legacy endures throughout the Gold Country. Bart politely but effectively carried out twenty-eight robberies before tripping up. His mode of operation was always the same. He waited alone, without even a getaway horse, along the road at an uphill spot where the stage horses slowed. His face was covered with a cloth flour sack that had holes cut for his eyes. Armed with a shotgun (which he never fired and which was later found to be empty) Bart quietly asked the stage driver, "Would you throw down your treasure box, sir?" Bart never disturbed the passengers, except for collecting all their firearms; his one grudge was with Wells Fargo, a company he taunted with doggerel. He carried a blanket roll with an ax in it. With that ax, Bart would cut open the strong box, remove the loot, and somehow disappear on foot into the woods. On his twenty-ninth robbery attempt, a passenger who had been let off the stage to do some hunting surprised Bart as he was opening the treasure box. Bart disappeared, but he dropped a handkerchief with his identifying laundry mark, which was traced to a San Francisco laundry.

The Sierra Repertory Theatre performs at the Fallon House. Columbia is a major festival site in the Gold Country, with the most prominent annual event, a Fireman's Muster, occurring in May. During the muster you can see old fire-fighting equipment. The passionate practitioners of old-time fire-fighting skills compete against one another in bucket brigades, water pumping contests, ladder raisings, and hose-cart relays. Fire was a constant worry in the tinder-dry, wooden Gold Rush towns. Other festivals here are the Columbia Diggins living-history program in June, a July 4 Celebration, and a Miner's Christmas.

If you have time to visit only a single Gold Country place besides the Gold Discovery site at Coloma, start with Columbia. In 1854 the town had four banks, eight hotels, two fire companies, fifty-three stores, and forty saloons.

Beyond Columbia, the pleasure of the Gold Country is partly that it rambles in an undefined manner, perfect for the explorer temperament of many travelers. Many discoveries await the visitor like hidden nuggets. Here are a few to whet your appetite as you drive Highway 49:

Jamestown boasts a special rail attraction from the post–Gold Rush era. Railtown 1897 State Historic Park (209–984–3953) includes steam locomotives and cars from the Sierra Railway Company. You can board the train, the *Mother Lode Cannonball,* for an hour-long scenic ride along 12 miles of track in an oak-laden terrain.

In Mariposa you can see trophy gold nuggets and other stunning state minerals at the California State Mining and Mineral Museum (209–742–7625). This lavish collection of the state's gold and other mineral specimens languished for decades in the Ferry Building along the San Francisco waterfront. Now it is installed in handsome quarters just south of Mariposa at the County Fairgrounds. The collection benefits both from the aesthetic sense of an appropriate locale for mineral celebration, the Gold Country, and from a decent, modern display space.

The collection includes some of the finest examples of gold nuggets found in California, such as the 203-ounce Fricot nugget. California leads all states in nonfuel mineral extraction, amounting to some $3 billion per year. The collection boasts museum-quality specimens in all mineral categories. So vast is the collection that only about 10 percent of it is actually on view. Begun in the 1880s, the collection's mandate is "to acquire, catalog, and display the important minerals of California."

At Jackson you can see two huge wooden wheels used to carry buckets of water and debris from the Kennedy Mine. Originally there were four such wheels in place, each 58 feet in diameter. Together they could carry 500 tons of water and debris from the mines each day. The wheels can be seen at a park north of Jackson on Jackson Gate Road. The Kennedy and Argonaut Mines, among the richest and deepest in the Mother Lode, produced about $60 million in gold.

Architecturally, the Chew Kee Store in Fiddletown is unusual because it is of rammed-earth construction. The walls are 2½ feet thick. Built in 1850, the structure was a Chinese herb shop and home of Fiddletown's last Chinese resident, Jimmy Chow, until his death in 1965.

Getting there

Reach Columbia, which is on Highway 49, by taking Interstate 580 east from the Bay Area to Tracy, then Highway 120 east to Highway 49, the Gold Country highway. Turn north on 49 to Columbia, which is 3 miles north of Sonora.

Wells Fargo stagecoaches carried the gold from Columbia to the treasure houses of San Francisco.

Be sure to see

Amble around Columbia, looking for all the details mentioned here. Then pursue a couple of the other suggested stops.

Best time to visit

One of the most famous festivals in these parts is the Fireman's Muster in May at Columbia (call for exact date). Another contender is the annual Calaveras County Fair and Jumping Frog Jubilee, held the third weekend in May and drawing more than 5,000 people. The Jumping Frog Jubilee (209–736–0049) honors Mark Twain and his story "The Celebrated Jumping Frog of Calaveras County." You can visit the cabin (on Highway 49, 3 miles south of Angels Camp) where Twain lived while gathering California material for his stories. A statue at Angels Camp recalls the author, who came west with his brother, Orion, failed at mining, and took up the pen to earn his livelihood.

Summer is the busiest month; autumn offers the attractive colors of the red oak and yellow maple leaves. Spring entices with an outpouring of wildflowers and a cultivated show at one site, Daffodil Hill (13 miles from Sutter Creek via Shake Ridge Road).

Lodging

The historic City Hotel (P.O. Box 1870, Columbia, CA 95310; 800–532–1479; www.cityhotel.com) is a premier Gold Country hostelry. There are ten guest rooms furnished with antiques, plus another fourteen rooms in their sister hotel, Fallon House.

Dining

The dining room at the City Hotel in Columbia would be the place to eat. The culinary approach is French cuisine with California accents, emphasizing fresh, local ingredients. Try the rack of lamb and the lemon soufflé dessert.

For more information

There is a state historic park Web site for Columbia at www.cal-parks.ca.gov. Columbia State Historic Park headquarters is at 22708 Broadway, Columbia, CA 95310; (209) 532–0150.

Contact the chambers of commerce or designated visitor bureaus from the respective areas for more detailed information. Moving south to north, the resources are as follows:

Yosemite Sierra Visitors Bureau, 40637 Highway 41, Oakhurst, CA 93644; (559) 683–4636; www.go2yosemite.net.

Mariposa County Visitors Center, P.O. Box 967, Mariposa, CA 95338; (888) 554–9011; http://mariposa.yosemite.net/visitor.

Tuolumne County Visitors Bureau, P.O. Box 4020, Sonora, CA 95370; (800) 446–1333; www.thegreatunfenced.com.

Calaveras Visitors Bureau, P.O. Box 637, Angels Camp, CA 95222; (800) 225–3764; www.visitcalaveras.org.

Amador County Chamber of Commerce, 125 Peek Street, Suite B, Jackson, CA 95642; (800) 649–4988; amadorcountychamber.com.

El Dorado County Chamber of Commerce, 542 Main Street, Placerville, CA 95667; (800) 457–6279; www.eldoradocounty.org.

Placer County Visitor Information Center, 13464 Lincoln Way, Auburn, CA 95603; (800) 427–6463; www.placer.ca.gov.

Grass Valley/Nevada County Chamber of Commerce, 248 Mill Street, Grass Valley, CA 95945; (800) 655–4667; www.gvncchamber.org.

35

Sacramento and the Gold Country

Gold Rush Serendipity: Places and Legends

The gold miner was an explorer—willing to go off the beaten path, alert for information but also willing to follow a hunch, knowing there were many treasures to be found. Today you can mine the travel treasures of the Gold Country for yourself.

The historic story

Here are just a few of the places and legends that a traveler with an interest in history will savor rambling up and down Highway 49 in the Gold Country.

Placerville was a major supply site for the miners, and several famous captains of industry had their humble beginnings here. Railroad magnate Mark Hopkins sold vegetables. Philip Armour ran a butcher shop. John Studebaker ran a wheelbarrow shop, amassing capital for larger ventures. Collis P. Huntington, later a rail tycoon, managed a store here.

Nevada City is another pleasant Gold Country town to poke around in. You'll stumble across the Nevada City Winery, known for its Zinfandel. Next door is the Miner's Foundry, a museum with foundry equipment but now also transformed into a performing arts venue.

On Main Street you'll happen on the Firehouse, a redbrick building from 1861. So numerous and fearful were fires that fire prevention societies became a leading social force in the early Gold Country era. Down the street is Nevada City Angler, heaven for the trout fisher, where guide service, flies, and all sorts of fly-fishing paraphernalia can be enjoyed.

At the end of Main Street is the historic National Hotel and Bar, the longest continuously operating hotel in California. You might stop for a drink at this dark wood bar and admire its collection of mixed-drink shakers. Nevada City is also known for its Victorian mansions, such as the Ott House (450 Broad Street). Nevada City prides itself on what its historic district lacks—no turn signals, no neon. The streetlamps are still actual gas lamps.

Antiques hunters will be delighted by the numerous stores selling varied wares throughout the Gold Country. Jackson has several antiques stores. Because of the patronage from travelers, many artists are also located in the Gold Country and sell directly to visitors.

Victorian architecture in churches and residences could be another focus of a Gold Country excursion. The red St. James Episcopal Church (1859) in Sonora and the Bradford House across the street are both fine examples of Gold Rush Victorian architecture. Sonora residents have organized a Sonora Heritage Home Tour. Brochures and maps are available locally.

Grass Valley offers a self-guided architectural walk. As you stroll the town, stop in at the historic Holbrooke Hotel (212 West Main Street), whose wooden bar is inviting and whose dining room is notable. One of the loveliest Victorian houses is the Frank Beatty residence (403 Neal Street).

Personalities have played a major role in the Gold Country legend. Aside from Mark Twain, two of the most colorful were entertainer Lola Montez and robber Black Bart.

Lola Montez, who flourished in Grass Valley, arrived from Europe, where she had been the mistress of Ludwig of Bavaria, among others. Her "salon" in Grass Valley was the place to enjoy polite company. It is said that Lola kept grizzly cubs as pets. Famed as a beauty and singer, she intrigued miners with her notorious Spider Dance, during which fake cork spiders were shaken from her dress. While walking Grass Valley be sure to see the Lola Montez House (248 Mill Street), which is now the visitor center for the region.

Getting there

The Gold Country stretches all along Highway 49. Valuable travel nuggets can be found everywhere.

Be sure to see

Any of the subjects mentioned above would be intriguing to explore.

Best time to visit

Autumn is a particularly congenial time to explore the Gold Country because the crowds have thinned and the leaves have turned color.

Nevada City is known for its choice Victorian homes,
including the Ott House.

Lodging

Every town up and down the Gold Country route has its own interesting hotel. Volcano's St. George Hotel (P.O. Box 9, Volcano, CA 95689; 209–296–4458; www.stgeorgehotel.com) is a handsome three-story brick structure from 1862 with wooden balconies and an abundant collection of historic items.

Dining

The local hotel often operates a fine dining room. The St. George in Volcano also has a lively bar, and the proprietor is the restaurant's chef. The St. George is a B&B, so breakfast is included.

For more information

See chapter 34 for listings of the Gold Country chambers of commerce and visitors bureaus.

36

Sacramento and the Gold Country

Small Museums in the Gold Country: Chaw Se to Auburn

The small museums of the Gold Country tell a thousand stories, not all of them pretty—especially for those not certified as white Americans. Take a walk through the light and dark sides of Gold Rush history.

The historic story

The actual world of the Gold Rush was a time of hardship, fueled by the vision of a Mother Lode of rich ore-bearing earth. But for every lucky miner, a hundred failed. Miners were willing to endure hours of tedious work in icy Sierra streams to secure a few nuggets. Costs were high, with a slice of bread going for a dollar, a shirt for $50, and a plain shovel for as much as $100. The enduring wealth of the mining era rested in the pockets of shopkeepers, who could charge what the market would bear for their goods. Many illustrious California names, such as Mark Hopkins, started their fortunes here selling hardware and vegetables.

Miners from other countries played major roles in the development of the Gold Country and the West in general, but prejudice and avarice combined as white Americans physically forced or taxed off the Mexican, Chilean, and Chinese miners.

Mexican miners from the state of Sonora, with their considerable experience in silver mining, were among the first to work the southern area of the Gold Country. The names Sonora and Mariposa, Spanish for butterfly, testify to their presence. In 1856 the mining town of Chinese Camp was populated with about 5,000 Chinese miners, who later became the workforce that built the railroads over the Sierra.

Now the setting is tranquil, the small towns pride themselves on their underdeveloped status, and you can almost feel cares slough off as you drive through the Sierra foothills.

One special outdoor museum honors the Native Americans who lived here before the Gold Rush. Everyone interested in the Native American contribution should pause at Chaw Se, or Indian Grinding Rock State Historic Park (209–296–7488). The park, on the road connecting Pine Grove with Volcano, off Highway 88, is the only state park devoted to Indian culture. Here you'll see how Indians ground acorns into meal for hundreds of years, using mortars in 1,185 mortar cups (the chaw-ses) they wore in a huge limestone rock. Large valley oaks, once the major food producers, dominate the landscape. While women processed the acorns, the men hunted for deer in this western Sierra location. Bark tepeelike structures re-create what the Indians lived in. Acorns, roughly half the Indian diet, were cooked by dropping hot rocks into baskets filled with water and acorn meal. Because of the need for watertight baskets, basket-making was one of the most advanced skills among Indians in California. Another fascinating aspect of Chaw Se is the 383 rock carvings, or petroglyphs, carved into the rock, perhaps representing the carver's thoughts on the desire for a good hunt, the cycle of life, or the coming of age. Some of these carvings are estimated to be 2,000 to 3,000 years old. A regional Indian museum exhibits artifacts from the ten tribes of the Sierra region. Only a few Indians survived the onslaught of gold miners and blended into the new culture.

There are many small museums throughout Gold Country, each supported by its local community. They could absorb several days of your attention. Here are some choices:

The Mariposa Museum and History Center (209–966–2924), Twelfth and Jessie Streets in Mariposa, includes a stamp mill used to crush rock in search of gold, a monitor nozzle, and several horse-drawn vehicles from the mining era. While in town be sure to see the stately Mariposa County Courthouse, the oldest courthouse still in use in California. The white-frame structure was built in 1854 and cost $12,000. You can tour the inside, including the courtroom with its original furniture.

The Tuolumne County Museum and History Center (209–532–1317), on West Bradford Avenue in Sonora, was once the county jail. Like many Gold Country structures, it was consumed by flames in the 1850s and then rebuilt. Fire was the scourge of the hastily built wooden mining towns, which explains why the fire company was such an important civil and social entity. The museum, which has an outstanding gold nugget collection, also shows period clothing and historic photographs as well as the restored jail.

You can see bark tepees similar to those once used by Native Americans at Indian Grinding Rock State Historic Park.

The Calaveras County Museum (209–754–3918), 30 North Main Street in San Andreas, is located in the county courthouse where the infamous bandit Black Bart was tried, convicted, and jailed. You can visit the jail cell where Bart spent four years before being tranferred to San Quentin to serve out the remainder of the six-year term he was given for the final robbery, the only one for which he was convicted.

The Amador County Museum (209–223–6386), on Church Street in Jackson, resides in the historic Brown House, a brick structure from 1859. The museum's tour de force is an intricate working scale model of local mine structures. Among the museum holdings are period clothing, household utensils, furniture, musical instruments, and literary evidence of mining-era culture. The men who came to California to the mines were often the educated and prosperous sons of strong families. Sometimes the second son, who could not inherit the family land or business, was sent to seek his fortune in California.

The El Dorado County Historical Museum (530–621–5865), at the county fairgrounds west of Placerville, boasts a restored Wells Fargo stagecoach, plus a re-creation of a turn-of-the-century store and kitchen. At the El Dorado County Museum, many of the holdings can be seen outdoors. The artifacts include a bark tepee structure such as the local Nisean Indians lived in, old and rusted mining equipment, aging stage coaches, and railroad cars in various stages of disintegration.

The Placer County Historical Museum (530–889–6500) in Auburn is housed in an architectural gem of the Gold Country, the Placer County Courthouse. This gold-domed structure stands forth regally, as befits the town through which the Central Pacific Railroad headed east into the mountains. Within the museum, be sure to see the gold nugget display in the gift shop and the elaborate Indian basketry displayed in several cases. If a docent is on duty, ask to be shown the historic Sheriff's Office, which is kept locked. Inside, you'll see the jail ledgers that recorded the names of all those incarcerated, including a line describing their offense. Beyond the Courthouse, stroll Auburn to see its antiques stores and the statue to Claude Chama, the town's founding miner.

Getting there

All these towns are along Highway 49.

Be sure to see

The listed museums, organized south to north, are treasures awaiting you. Include a stop at Chaw Se, the Native American state historic park.

Best time to visit

The Gold Country is a year-round destination. The Big Time celebration at Chaw Se in September is a good time to learn about the Miwok and other tribes.

Lodging

Many historic buildings that were hotels during the Gold-Rush era continue to function as such. The Hotel Leger (8304 Main Street, Mokelumne Hill, CA 95245; 209–286–1401), built in 1851, was originally called the Hotel de France.

Dining

The local dining room in the town's historic hotel is often your best bet. The Hotel Leger is noted for its steaks, Friday night Mexican dinners, and weekend brunches.

For more information

See chapter 34 for listings of the Gold Country chambers of commerce and visitors bureaus. Chaw Se has a Web site at www.cal-parks.ca.gov.

37

Sacramento and the Gold Country

The Richest Mine and Environmental Original Sin: The Empire Mine and Malakoff Diggins

In the latter days of the Gold Rush, the big money lay in expensive deep-rock mining. Those without deep pockets resorted to hydraulic mining—an environmental disaster that led to wars between miners and farmers. Visit the sites of the richest and the worst of them all.

The historic story

The Empire Mine State Historic Park, site of the richest gold mine in California (5.8 million ounces), is intriguing both for what you see and what you don't see. Above ground at this Grass Valley location, you can gaze upon some marvelous examples of gold in quartz rock at the visitor center. Outside, you stroll the landscaped grounds of mine owner William Bourn. The architectural gem is Bourn's "Empire Cottage," a sumptuous stone building designed by noted architect Willis Polk. Adjacent to the Cottage is a rose garden with specimens of roses developed from ancient times to 1929. Aboveground you can view the remains of the mining apparatus, the machine shops and the stamp mill, used here for 106 years of operations. You can peer a few feet into the shaft of the mine, where the miners went down and the ore came out. The mineshaft is closed to the public.

What you don't see—but what you can envision after you have viewed a scale model of the underground mine in the visitor center—are the 367 miles of tunnels, sometimes descending over a mile deep and sprawling at all levels over a 5-square-mile area.

Hydraulic mining washed away hillsides at Malakoff Diggins State Historic Park.

The story of the Empire Mine is a tale of the later phase of the Gold Country saga, when the serious gold remaining to be found lay in deep-rock veins requiring massive capital to exploit. The secretly built model of all the underground tunnels was constructed by mine engineers for the express purpose of determining the veins of gold and plotting where to tunnel next. Color-coded wire indicates the relative richness of the ore in each tunnel. Once you've viewed the model, you can appreciate the mazelike unseen belowground world.

If Empire was indeed *the* gold mine, Malakoff was the true environmental original sin.

Malakoff Diggins State Historic Park, 26 miles northeast of Nevada City, is the scar and the eyesore of the Gold Country—visually, historically, and spiritually. In fact, this park serves as an example of the most environmentally degrading activities of man in California. You can get there via Tyler-Foote Crossing Road from Highway 49.

Malakoff was the world's largest hydraulic gold mine. Huge nozzles, called monitors, were connected with elaborate ditches and flumes that diverted mountain streams. The nozzles blasted away at the gravel hillsides, washing down the soil. The washed pit at Malakoff is fully 7,000 feet long and 3,000 feet wide. As the gravel washed through sluices, the heavier gold could be separated. The environmental disaster was caused by tons of the silt that remained in the water and proceeded downstream. Farms were flooded by clogged rivers as streambeds filled with silt. Hydraulic mining was ended by court order in 1884.

Today the park encompasses 3,000 acres of oak woodlands, pine forests, and meadows. The white wooden buildings of the North Bloomfield town-site, located in the park, have been restored and refurnished to show what life was like here in the 1870s.

Getting there

Drive east from San Francisco on Interstate 80, passing north of Sacramento. Continue on Interstate 80 until you reach Highway 49, then turn north to Grass Valley (home of the Empire Mine) and continue on 49 to the Malakoff Diggins. Eight miles of the road to Malakoff are unpaved and winding, so allow plenty of time. The Empire Mine could absorb a half day of time; Malakoff would require a full day to explore.

Be sure to see

The Empire Mine is in Grass Valley; Malakoff Diggins is to the north.

Best time to visit

Summer is definitely the best season to visit these parks because their resources are up and running. The gravel road into Malakoff is passable in the dry season, more chancy in the wet of winter.

Lodging

Because of its fine Victorian homes, the Gold Country has come prime B&B territory for the California explorer. One good example of such lodgings in Grass Valley is as Murphy's Inn (318 Neal Street, Grass Valley, CA 95945; 530–273–6873; www.murphysinn.com). The house itself is architecturally interesting and dates from 1866, when Edward Coleman flourished in the mining and logging business.

Dining

One good Italian eatery in Grass Valley is Pasta Luigi's (760 South Auburn Street; 530–477–0455). The food is tasty, the atmosphere pleasant but unpretentious, and the prices offer good value. Try the linguini zingarella, a flat-noodle pasta with spicy sausage and sun-dried tomatoes.

For more information

Contact Empire Mine State Historic Park at 10791 East Empire Street, Grass Valley; (530) 273–8522. Malakoff Diggins State Historic Park is 16 miles northeast of Nevada City on North Bloomfield Road; call (530) 265–2740. Both have Web sites at www.cal-parks.ca.gov.

38

Sacramento and the Gold Country

Meandering the California Delta: The Chinese Town of Locke

Fighting discrimination at every turn, some Chinese formed their own town on the California Delta. You can still find a few Chinese merchants in Locke, as well as a museum with artifacts of the town's heyday. Then tour other small towns along the Sacramento River, reminders of rural California—and the enduring wealth of agriculture.

The historic story

The gold era was brief, only a few years for picking nuggets out of streams and a few decades for blasting gold-bearing quartz belowground. The former was a democratic chance for any man to strike it rich, and some did—though a hundred died of pneumonia from exposure in the cold mountain streams for every one who earned riches. The latter approach required vast capitalization, leaving the little man out.

Some of those who didn't strike it rich in the gold fields turned to agriculture to sustain themselves. In California's agricultural abundance lay a wealth exponentially beyond the dollar value of gold. Nowhere is this more apparent than in the leisurely drives possible on the Delta levees, where pear orchards, sorghum plantings, and sugar beet crops stretch before you.

The Delta—where the Sacramento, Mokelumne, and San Joaquin Rivers converge before flowing into San Francisco Bay—is the northwest end of the Great Central Valley of California, easily one of the most productive agricultural regions on the planet. Between Bakersfield in the south and Stockton in the north astonishing amounts of tomatoes, almonds, apricots, cotton, grapes,

The Delta

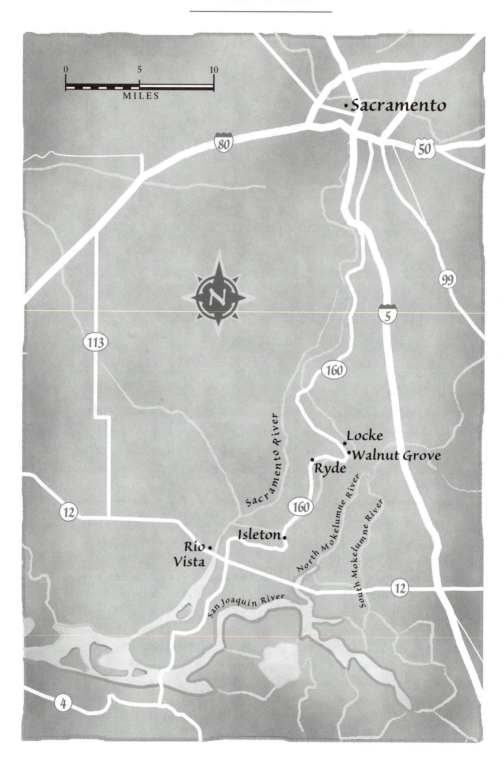

walnuts, and asparagus are grown here.

The remarkable reality of the Delta is that levees have been built to create fifty-five man-made "islands," impounding some 550,000 acres of arable land against the seasonal high water. The Delta levee construction began in the 1850s and accelerated in the 1870s with the invention of the clamshell dredge, which could scoop up riverbottom materials and deposit them ashore. By the 1930s the full pattern of Delta levees had been completed.

The Chinese made major contributions to California, first mining for gold, then building the railroad across the Sierra, and finally helping to construct the Delta levees and settling in as farmers. The town of Locke in the Delta was founded entirely by Chinese in 1916 after fire destroyed the Chinatown area of nearby Walnut Grove. The burned-out Chinese leased the land from George and Clay Locke and set out to create houses and shops.

Locke once boasted a theater, six restaurants, and a fluctuating number of brothels, but it is now a mere ghost of its former flourishing life, with about fifty residents. You can visit the Dai Loy Chinese Museum, once a gambling hall, to see photos and artifacts about the everyday life of the Chinese here. The River Road Art Gallery shows a range of artists who live and create in the Delta. Al's Place, a rough-hewn saloon and restaurant, serves up beverages and steaks. At Al's Place the ceiling is littered with fading dollar bills. The buildings of Locke linger in a state of arrested decay, narrowly resisting the urge to collapse.

Beyond wandering Locke's streets, another enjoyable excursion here is meandering up and down the roads on both banks of the Sacramento River around Locke. Highway 160 is the main roadway.

For the traveler the charm of the Delta lies in the small towns along the river. The town of Rio Vista, for example, has a concentration of wealth from its early days as a shipping center and its present role as a leader in agricultural and natural gas production.

In Rio Vista you'll see a special monument to an event in 1985. A wayward humpback whale, affectionately named Humphrey, swam all the way upriver to Rio Vista and made the area his home until he could be escorted back to the open ocean.

People in the small Delta towns are a gregarious mix of hyphenated Americans, especially Portuguese, Italians, and Filipinos. Though their lives are usually passed in such sober pursuits as raising food crops, running resorts, and tending shops, Delta people possess a streak of eccentricity. Foster's Bighorn Cafe in Rio Vista displays a famous collection of mounted big game from Africa, Asia, and the Americas.

One interesting Delta trip is the 20-mile Tyler Loop out of Walnut

The Ryde Hotel was a fashionable waystop for riverboats
along the Sacramento River.

Grove, which you can make by car, bicycle, or boat. You'll pass Georgiana
Slough—one of the most beautiful Delta waterways—lined with willow,
poplar, and oak. Fields of wheat, corn, barley, and other crops stretch in every
direction.

Getting there

Locke is along Highway 160, which runs along the banks of the Sacramento
River. The drive is an hour northeast of San Francisco.

Be sure to see

Locke is the main stop, but other Delta towns on either side of the Sacramento River are also of interest.

Best time to visit

The Delta is a good destination any time of year. Isleton hosts a popular
Crawdad Festival in June.

Lodging

Originally built in 1927 as a waystop for riverboats, the Ryde Hotel (14340 Highway 160, P.O. Box 43, Ryde, CA 95680; 916–776–1318; www.rydehotel.com) is now a bright spot in the Delta scene.

Dining

The Ryde Hotel dining room comes alive on the weekends for casual lunches and fine-dining evenings with jazz accompanying the menu of chicken, fresh fish, fillets, and pasta. There is also a Sunday champagne brunch.

For more information

Contact the California Delta Chamber of Commerce at P.O. Box 6, Isleton, CA 95641; (916) 777–5007; www.californiadelta.org. For a free e-mail newsletter about the Delta—titled *California Delta Scuttlebutt,* managed by longtime enthusiast Hal Schell—send a blank e-mail to calif-delta-on@mail-list.com.

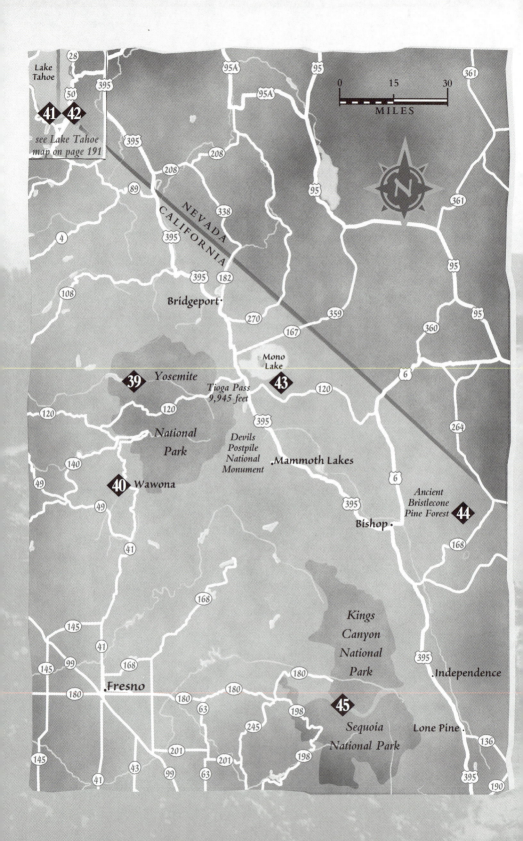

see Lake Tahoe
map on page 191

41 **42**

Lake
Tahoe

28

50

395

395

89

4

108

95A

95A

208

208

338

395

395

182

Bridgeport·

270

167

359

95

95

95

361

361

95

360

6

0   15   30

MILES

N

39 Yosemite

Tioga Pass
9,945 feet

Mono
Lake

43

120

120

395

National

Park

Devils
Postpile
National
Monument

·Mammoth Lakes

264

6

140

49

40 ·Wawona

Ancient
Bristlecone
Pine Forest

44

395

Bishop·

168

49

41

168

145

41

168

99

Kings

Canyon

National

Park

395

·Independence

145

99

·Fresno

180

180

180

63

198

45

Sequoia

National Park

·Independence

Lone Pine·

136

145

201

245

41

43

99

63

201

198

395

190

The Sierra

39

The Sierra

The Discovery and Saving of Yosemite: A Militiaman's Emotions

"As I looked, a peculiar sensation seemed to fill my whole being, and I found my eyes in tears with emotion." The year was 1851, and the observer was not a poet but a simple militiaman. Share his sense of awe as you view the wonders of Yosemite National Park.

The historic story

The simple eloquence of that rough militiaman testifies to the universal experience of Yosemite, a mountain retreat of awesome beauty in east central California. So many travelers when first encountering Yosemite Valley, an 8-mile funnel with a flat base and 3,000-foot granite walls, feel the same sense of subdued grandeur about the place—a sense of nature's cathedral, a spare and ennobling aura.

In 1864 Abraham Lincoln signed a bill, the Yosemite Grant to California, authorizing state protection of Yosemite Valley and the giant sequoias of the area. Spurred by pleas and publicity from John Muir and others, Yosemite National Park was legislated in 1890. Later, on a famous camping trip, Teddy Roosevelt visited Yosemite with John Muir. The trip energized Roosevelt to create a record-breaking number of public parks and monuments during his presidency.

The history of major interest in Yosemite is not the mere human time frame but the geological story. Over eons the forces of glacial activity have scraped away at the granite rock, exposing the faces, such as El Capitan and Half Dome, that stun the imagination with their size. The rushing Merced River has carried rock fragments and silt from higher mountain areas to the floor of the valley. Prior to the glacial periods Yosemite was a sea, with extensive sedimentary deposits. Gradually, geological forces of uplift thrust the seabed to its present elevation.

Miwok and Mono Lake Paiute Indians established villages along the Merced River, which runs through Yosemite Valley. The Native Americans called the Valley "Ahwahnee," which apparently meant "gaping mouth." They may have lived here for several thousand years, gathering acorns and seeds, fishing for trout, and hunting deer. Except for a period around 1800 when a disease known as "the fatal black sickness" forced them out of the area, the Native Americans lived peacefully within the Yosemite Valley. Not until much later, after the Gold Rush, did white men stumble upon the area. Today you can see living demonstrations of life in a Miwok village; these take place at the park's visitor center and are performed by descendants of the original Miwoks, making this event a highlight of a Yosemite trip. You'll see how the Miwoks harvested the black oak acorns, hunted for deer, and lived in bark structures.

Getting there

The most direct routes to Yosemite Valley from San Francisco are Highway 120 east from Manteca or Highway 132 at the Modesto turnoff from Interstate 5–580. The all-weather gateway to Yosemite is Merced, a town in the Great Central Valley of California. From Merced take Highway 140 east into Yosemite Valley. Merced is about three hours by car from San Francisco. Allow another hour for the drive along narrow, winding roads to the park. Amtrak is a relaxing way to get to Yosemite. The train arranges bus transportation into Yosemite Valley from Merced.

Be sure to see

Start at the visitor center, where you'll find an excellent selection of guidebooks and maps, plus a ranger to suggest outings. Some favorite initial outings are easy to make with the help of a ranger's directions.

Visit the site where John Muir showed Theodore Roosevelt the wonder of Yosemite during their famous encampment here. A marker on the valley floor recalls the event.

Drive or tram around the valley to view all the different falls. Yosemite Falls dominates the scenery. Upper Yosemite drops 1,430 feet in one abrupt fall; the Lower Falls drop another 320 feet.

Walk up to Mirror Lake. The walk is lovely and the setting, an alpine lake quickly silting due to natural succession, illustrates the geologic forces still at work today.

Inspiration Point at Yosemite presents a classic view of El Capitan and Half Dome.

Walk up to Nevada Falls. Part of the pleasure of this walk are the ever-changing vistas of such familiar landmarks as Yosemite Falls and Half Dome.

Yosemite Valley, which 90 percent of park visitors never leave, is only a miniscule part of Yosemite National Park. The valley represents only 7 of the park's total 1,169 square miles. There are 196 miles of primary roads and about 800 miles of trail to entice you beyond Yosemite Valley. Make an effort to get out of the valley to Wawona to see the sequoias, or get to the high country to see Tuolumne Meadows, a rocky alpine wilderness. Highway 120, the Tioga Pass Road, is closed in winter.

Best time to visit

Each season brings its own special rewards to a Yosemite visitor. Summer offers the most active historic interpretive programs and best access to roads in the high country.

Lodging

The historic lodging in Yosemite Valley is the Ahwahnee, one of the most distinctive lodgings in any national park. See below for the contact information.

Dining

For a memorable experience dine at the venerable Ahwahnee Dining Room.

For more information

Contact Yosemite Concession Services–Reservation at 5410 East Home Avenue, Fresno, CA 93727; (559) 252–4848; www.yosemitepark.com. They manage all park information and reservations and will send you a brochure on the park, including accommodation information.

For recorded park information, call (209) 372–1000.

The park service can be reached by writing the Superintendent, P.O. Box 577, Yosemite National Park, CA 95389; (209) 372–0200. Yosemite's Web site is www.nps.gov/yose.

40

The Sierra

Yosemite's Wawona: An Historic Hotel and the Big Trees

Wawona—a special world unto itself in southern Yosemite—
was the first stagecoach route into the park. You can still stay at
the hotel where all the stages stopped and steep yourself in the
area's living history, including a magnificent stand of the coast
redwoods' inland cousins.

The historic story

Wawona was one of John Muir's favorite places. Born in Scotland and educated in botany at the University of Wisconsin, Muir ended up in California,
where the Sierra was his main terrain of meditation. Muir's books *My First
Summer in the Sierra* and *The Yosemite* make fitting literary companions for a
trip to the park.

On the way to Wawona from the Valley Floor, make one detour to the
viewpoint on the road up Glacier Point. The turnoff, just before the Wawona
Tunnel, presents one of the most famous vistas in the park, rivaling the view
from Glacier Point. From this elevated position you'll enjoy a sweeping
panorama of all major landforms in the valley, and you'll acquire an excellent
perspective of the glacial forces that scoured out the upper part of the valley,
peeling off the granite layers from the mountains as if they were the layers of
an onion, and depositing a moraine of rocky debris at the western end. Three
successive waves of glaciers slid across the granite face of Yosemite, polishing
Half Dome and El Capitan to their present smoothness; the most recent glacier retreated only 10,000 years ago.

Then proceed on to Wawona. The *Sequoiadendron giganteums*, the Big

Trees, can be seen at three groves in Yosemite. The most prominent, Mariposa Grove, lies 35 miles south of the valley along Highway 41 in Wawona, which means "big tree" in the original Native American language. The giant sequoias are the inland species of redwoods, the most massive living entities on the earth. They are worth a half-day trip to Wawona to see. The largest example of the inland redwood, the General Sherman Tree, is farther south along the mountains in Sequoia National Park.

In the Wawona-area grove, the Grizzly Giant is the oldest tree, at an estimated 2,800 years, and has a base diameter of 30.7 feet. Nearby, the Massachusetts Tree, broken into chunks, shows the wood of the sequoia. There used to be two tunnel trees in Wawona, but one, the Wawona Tunnel Tree, fell over in 1968-69 winter storms. The 232-foot California Tree remains upright; however, cars are no longer allowed to drive in the grove, which can now be seen on foot or by tram.

The Wawona area is rich in history. The venerable Wawona Hotel, with its weekend barbecues, and the nearby Pioneer Yosemite History Center, describing the life of early homesteaders in ten restored building, are among the resources at Wawona.

The Wawona Hotel is a grand, white wooden structure, which includes some very early construction, such as the 1877 Clark Cottage. In the lobby you'll find historic photos of the Thomas Hill studio, which is nearby. You'll also see a photo of John Muir and Teddy Roosevelt at the Grizzly Giant tree in the Wawona grove. One special pleasure of the Wawona Hotel is entertainer Tom Bopp, who has made a career out of sharing early Yosemite lore and song in his evening shows in the hotel's parlor.

The Pioneer Yosemite History Center is particularly pleasing in summer when costumed reenactors portray early life in Yosemite. Each building represents a different aspect of Yosemite history. The Covered Bridge and Grey Barn recalls that Wawona was the largest stage stop in Yosemite. All Yosemite-bound traffic crossed the bridge, which was built in 1857 by Galen Clark. The Artist Building highlights the fact that many artists were drawn to Yosemite for inspiration. Painter Christian Jorgenson constructed this building on the banks of the Merced River in Yosemite Valley. The Anderson Building salutes how tourist parties provided business for local residents. George Anderson, a miner and blacksmith, worked as a guide here in the 1800s. In 1875 he was the first man to climb Half Dome.

Getting there

Wawona is in the southern part of the park. If you are already in the park, follow the park road south from the Valley Floor to Wawona. Alternatively,

Wawona Hotel was the original stage stop for travelers entering Yosemite.

enter from the south via Highway 41, which meets Highway 49 south of Mariposa.

Be sure to see

Visit the historic Wawona Hotel and its lobby, filled with historic photos. See the Pioneer Yosemite History Center and linger around the historic structures, learning the story of early Yosemite.

Then take in the giant sequoias at the Mariposa Grove in Wawona. To adequately protect the trees, you must now venture in on foot or take a park service tram. The setting is impressive. Some of these arboreal giants are more than 300 feet high and 3,000 years old.

Best time to visit

Summer is definitely the best time to visit Wawona. In winter the lodging is open only on weekends and the big trees are accessible only on showshoes. The Pioneer Yosemite History Center is only staffed with reenactors in summer.

Lodging

The venerable Wawona Hotel (209–375–6556 for front desk; 559–252–4848 for reservations) is the place to stay.

Dining

The Wawona Hotel dining room serves breakfast, lunch, and dinner.

For more information

Contact Yosemite Concession Services–Reservation at 5410 East Home Avenue, Fresno, CA 93727; (559) 252–4848; www.yosemitepark.com. They manage all park information and reservations and will send you a brochure on the park, including accommodation information.

For recorded park information, call (209) 372–1000.

The park service can be reached by writing the Superintendent, P.O. Box 577, Yosemite National Park, CA 95389; (209) 372–0200. Yosemite's Web site is www.nps.gov/yose.

41

The Sierra

The Fairest Picture the Whole Earth Affords: Pioneers at Lake Tahoe

> Mark Twain, a man not given to easy superlatives, felt that Lake Tahoe was worthy of exception. He called it "the fairest picture the whole earth affords . . . The water is purer than the air, and the air is the air that angels breathe." Come up with your own superlatives as you tour the lake and sites of historic resorts by car, boat, or on foot.

The historic story

The main historic story about Tahoe concerns preservation of this remarkable treasure, including the tale of the lake's earlier users and the ongoing major development of the recent period.

Clarity (97 percent pure), deep bluish color, elevation (6,229 feet), mountainous and wooded setting in the Sierra Nevada, and size (22 miles long and 8 to 12 miles wide) combine to make Lake Tahoe one of the most attractive freshwater lakes in North America. The extraordinary blue color is caused by the lake's remarkable depth—as deep as 1,636 feet, with about 1,000 feet as the average. This third-deepest lake in North America could cover a flat area equal to the size of California with 14 inches of water.

When John Fremont became one of the first Europeans to see the lake—in 1844—the area was sparsely populated by Washoe Indians. It is thought that the name Tahoe comes from a Washoe Indian word meaning "water in a high place" or "lake in the sky." The lake is indeed in the sky, easily the largest alpine lake in North America.

Appreciated in the summer for its hiking opportunities and natural

Lake Tahoe

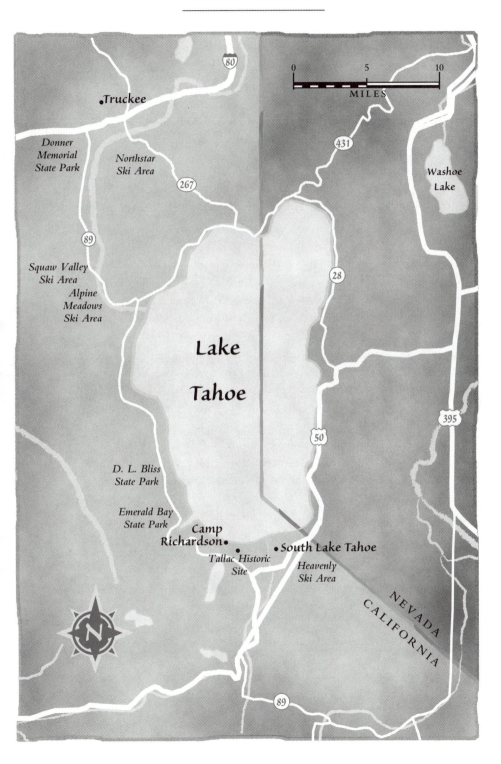

beauty and in winter for its ski areas, the Tahoe basin finds year-round enthusiasts. If you visit in spring or autumn, you'll find that the crowds have thinned.

The political struggle to achieve sensible but restrained development of the Tahoe area is an ongoing challenge. Ruining the natural beauty, overdrawing the available freshwater supply, and polluting the water purity are major concerns. The political decisions must be agreed upon by the two states, six counties, and perhaps twenty agencies with various authorities. A third of the lake rests in Nevada, with the rest in California. The lake nestles between the main north-south Sierra Nevada and an eastern offshoot, the Carson Range.

As early as 1870, Lake Tahoe flourished as a resort, where tycoon Elias J. "Lucky" Baldwin built a sizable lodge and took guests around the lake in his steamer. Early visitors caught legendary numbers of trout.

You can glimpse this early history at the Tallac Historic Site along the southwest edge of the lake. The Forest Service maintains a visitor center at Taylor Creek, a half mile from the Tallac Site, which interprets the human history of the region circa 1890–1920.

You can see the remaining foundations of Lucky Baldwin's Tallac Resort (1880–1920). One of the early homes, the Pope Estate (1894), has been restored and is used for historic interpretive programs. The Baldwin Estate (1921), home of Lucky's granddaughter, is now the Baldwin Museum, containing exhibits of Tahoe history. Adjacent to the estate is a Washoe Demonstration Garden, showing the plants and the bark structures the Washoe Indians used when passing the summer at Lake Tahoe. The Heller Estate (1923) serves as an events center. A Great Gatsby Festival in August brings alive this era and is a particularly congenial time for a visit. Each year the restoration of these homes becomes more complete as local volunteers advance historic interpretation.

After looking at the historic homes, tour the lake by car to enjoy the outdoor activities. The most celebrated scenic area is Emerald Bay, at the southwest corner of the lake. The contrast between the blue water and the mountains rising 3,000 feet over the lake has great appeal.

Beyond a car, excursion boats are an enjoyable way to experience the lake. The two main options are the *Tahoe Queen* (530–541–3364) and the MS *Dixie* (775–588–3508).

Across the lake, the nearby Nevada mining towns, where silver was the prize, are also interesting to explore. The main destination is Virginia City and the Comstock Lode, the silver bonanza discovered in 1859. After an intense decade of mining, the economic prosperity in the Tahoe region centered on

Emerald Bay entices with one of the loveliest views at Lake Tahoe.

lumber from 1870 to 1920. Tourism is the current major industry for both Virginia City and the city of Reno, with its gambling and entertainment. Carson City, the Nevada capital, is worth a stop to visit its elegant statehouse, history museum, and Victorian mansions.

Getting there

Lake Tahoe is about 200 miles (three and a half hours with the mountains) from San Francisco. To approach the north side of the lake, take Interstate 80, a somewhat easier drive on a divided highway with measured grades. However, you'll arrive at the north end, quite a drive from the south end's historic homes and scenery. To approach from the south, take Highway 50, a more demanding and curvy road, narrow in places. You'll arrive close to Emerald Bay and the Tallac Historic Site homes.

Be sure to see

The historic homes at the Tallac Historic Site at the southwest end of Lake Tahoe should be your first stop. Scenic Emerald Bay is a short drive north. The Rubicon Trail in Bliss State Park is one of the most pleasant walks in the Tahoe region, along a ridge above the lake. The Vikingsholm Trail in Bliss

Park is a steep 1-mile trail down to the water and an historic Scandinavian-style summer mansion, Vikingsholm, built in 1928.

Best time to visit

Summer, when lowland areas are hot, is the classic time to enjoy the cool mountain environment. The historic homes are open in summer and the interpretive program is alive, peaking during the Great Gatsby Festival in August.

Lodging

Lakeland Village (3535 Lake Tahoe Boulevard, South Lake Tahoe, CA 96150; 800–822–5969; www.lakeland-village.com) provides comfortable, lakefront condos at the south end of Lake Tahoe.

Dining

Evans (536 Emerald Bay Road, South Lake Tahoe; 530–542–1990) is the fine-dining leader of the Tahoe region. Try the mesclun lettuce salad with grilled portabello mushrooms as an appetizer and the roast swordfish on polenta as an entree.

For more information

For brochures and lodging prospects at the north end of the lake, contact the North Lake Tahoe Resort Association, Box 5459, Tahoe City, CA 96145; (800) 824–6348; www.tahoefun.org.

For south end information contact Lake Tahoe Visitors Authority, 1156 Ski Run Boulevard, South Lake Tahoe, CA 96150; (800) 288–2463; www. virtualtahoe.com.

The Forest Service is a major information source for historic interpretation and hiking in the Tahoe region, summer and winter. Summer headquarters is the Forest Service Visitor Center on Emerald Bay Road; (530) 573–2674. Year-round headquarters is at 870 Emerald Bay Road; (530) 573–2694.

42

The Sierra

From Snowshoe Thompson to the Squaw Valley Olympics: Story of California Skiing

The Squaw Valley Olympics of 1960 put Lake Tahoe on the map in the minds of millions of skiing enthusiasts. But you don't need to be a skier to enjoy the historic splendors of Lake Tahoe's ski areas. You don't even need to wait until winter— there's plenty to explore year-round.

The historic story

California offers some of the finest skiing in the world, especially at the major ski resorts in the Lake Tahoe basin.

Arguably, the greatest California skier of all time was a mailman named Snowshoe Thompson. Thompson, a Norwegian living in Sacramento, noticed that mail service to the silver miners in Nevada was suspended in winter because snow and ice locked up the Sierra. Snow had not stopped anyone in his native Norway, Thompson reckoned. So he fashioned 10-foot-long oak skis, balanced himself with a pole, and began carrying mail and supplies over the Sierra in winter for 50 cents per pound. It usually took him three days to go up the mountain and two days to get down. For more than twenty years Thompson kept up the service, making four trips per month, defying blizzards and avalanches. He always set forth on the appointed day in his announced schedule, regardless of weather conditions, carrying roughly one hundred pounds on his back.

Before the decision was made in the 1920s to keep Highway 80 open

Ice skaters enjoy a sunny afternoon at Squaw Valley.

year-round for national security purposes, skiing the California Sierras was restricted to hearty individuals like Thompson. Today all the ingredients necessary for an outstanding skiing experience are present around Lake Tahoe, with amenities that Snowshoe Thompson could never have imagined.

The snow usually falls plentifully, amounting to some 350 to 400 inches per year. Major ski areas have also invested in snowmaking equipment to give Mother Nature an assist in drought years. The ski season usually runs December to March.

The sun shows a welcome presence in California skiing. You are not likely to experience the long periods of bitter cold that characterize some inland skiing areas. Typically, a dazzling afternoon sun takes the chill off the early morning, creating an afternoon temperature of 25 to 45 degrees.

In many ways Badger Pass in Yosemite was the start of California skiing. Tourists there have gone skiing for the last hundred years, using primitive climbing and horse-drawn efforts to get themselves up the hills. Badger Pass correctly calls itself "California's Original Ski Resort," and ski lifts officially opened the area in 1935. But Badger Pass is small and does not have the expert runs that delight an advanced skier. Squaw Valley and the other major ski resorts in the Lake Tahoe basin meet those expectations.

Ever since the Winter Olympics were held at Squaw Valley in 1960, the popularity of skiing has increased in the Lake Tahoe basin. The panoramic view of one of the world's largest and clearest alpine lakes adds immensely to the aesthetic experience. The area has developed the greatest concentration of ski resorts in the United States. Fifteen Alpine ski resorts can be reached within a forty-five-minute drive of the lake; several of them also offer Nordic skiing, with groomed trails. Après-ski activities, both at the resorts and in the border towns, add a dimension of nightlife and culinary adventure to the region. Some resorts also function as summer destinations.

The major ski resorts are Northstar-at-Tahoe (800–466–6784; www. skinorthstar.com); Alpine Meadows (530–583–4232; www.skialpine.com); Squaw Valley (530–583–6985; www.squaw.com); Heavenly (775–586–7000; www.skiheavenly.com); Kirkwood (209–258–6000; www.skikirkwood.com); and Sierra-at-Tahoe (530–659–7453; www.sierratahoe.com).

Northstar is a self-contained condo environment with downhill skiing appropriate for all skill levels. Northstar has an elaborate Nordic or cross-country ski trail system.

Alpine Meadows is a family-oriented resort with the longest ski season in the Tahoe area. Notorious Scott's Chute is one of the steepest runs in skiing.

Squaw Valley, with its deserved reputation as a world-class ski area, offers night skiing on Friday and Saturday. The snowpack at Squaw Valley reaches about 450 inches per year.

Heavenly is America's largest ski resort, with nine mountains, a 3,500-foot drop, and 20 square miles of ski terrain.

Kirkwood, whose base is at 7,800 feet, features snow of the highest quality through all its runs. For Nordic skiers, Kirkwood offers 75 kilometers of groomed trails.

Sierra, with its location on the west side of Echo Summit, is the closest major resort to San Francisco or Sacramento. The view from the top of Sierra-at-Tahoe shows the Desolation Wilderness.

Nonskiers will enjoy a tram ride to the top of Heavenly or Squaw Valley, winter or summer, with a restaurant destination for libations or food to enjoy with the view. Both ski areas present outstanding views of Lake Tahoe from their elevated perspectives.

The most recent chapter in ski resort history concerns their summer use. Mountain biking has become a popular summer activity. You ride the tram to the top and let gravity pull you down the mountain. Hiking is also now popular in the highlands of the ski resorts.

Skiers and nonskiers alike enjoy the diversion that the Nevada side of the border offers at the gaming tables and entertainment in the casinos. This, too, is part of the historic story; Nevada first allowed gambling in 1931.

Getting there

Lake Tahoe ski areas are about three and a half hours from San Francisco. To approach the north side of the lake, take Interstate 80, a somewhat easier drive on a divided highway with measured grades. The north end has access to Northstar, Alpine Meadows, and Squaw Valley.

The northern approach also takes you through Truckee and Donner Lake, scene of the infamous Donner Party crossing of the Sierra in 1846. A contingent of wagon-train pioneers was caught in the Sierra by heavy snowfall that winter; some survived, partly by eating those who died—an event referred to in California history as The Donner Tragedy. The story is told at the Emigrant Trail Museum (530–582–7892) at Donner Lake. About 40,000 people traveled through the area on this trail to California in the pioneer period.

To approach from the south take Highway 50, a more demanding and curvy road that's narrow in places, especially when conditions are snowy or icy. En route you pass Sierra and arrive in South Lake Tahoe close to Heavenly. Another half-hour south and west is Kirkwood, via Highways 89 south and 88 west.

Be sure to see

Tour one or more of the major ski sites, winter or summer, whether you ski or just enjoy the mountain scenery. Take a ride to the top at either Heavenly or Squaw Valley for extraordinary views of Lake Tahoe.

Best time to visit

The ski areas are year-round destinations. Winter ski season is mainly December to March. Summer use is expanding, especially hiking and mountain biking.

Lodging

Historic Sorensen's (14255 Highway 88, Hope Valley, CA 96120; 800–423–9949; www.sorensensresort.com) is a cluster of cabins about twenty minutes from the south end of Lake Tahoe. Sorensen's is a good lodging choice if you want to concentrate your skiing or exploring on Heavenly and Kirkwood.

Dining

Sorensen's has its own restaurant. The gaming establishments at South Lake Tahoe, such as Harrah's, offer sumptuous buffet dinners at reasonable prices.

For more information

For information on the south end of Lake Tahoe, contact the Lake Tahoe Visitors Authority, 1156 Ski Run Boulevard, South Lake Tahoe, CA 96150; (800) 288–2463; www.virtualtahoe.com.

For north end information and lodging prospects, contact the North Lake Tahoe Resort Association, P.O. Box 5459, Tahoe City, CA 96145; (800) 824–6348; www.tahoefun.org.

43

The Sierra

East Side of the Sierra: Natural Beauty and the Struggle for Water

The treasures of the east side of the Sierra are a delight to explore. Underlying the beauty, however, is California's unending historic struggle over water. In fact, ensuring the very survival of such wonders as Mono Lake required judicial intervention.

The historic story

Partisans of California's Mammoth Lakes region in the eastern Sierra can argue persuasively that it competes for the honor of the most diverse outdoor summer region in the Golden State. However, behind the scenery is a long and bitter struggle over California resources, both water and real estate. About 75 percent of the state's water originates in Northern California, but about 75 percent of the water use is in Southern California. The survival of birds nesting at Mono Lake, for example, is due only to judicial intervention that required the Los Angeles Water District to keep water levels high enough to prevent predators from crossing to the bird-nesting islands in the lake.

The historic story begins in the early 1900s, when the City of Los Angeles Department of Water and Power built the Los Angeles Aqueduct and began to wrestle water rights away from Owens Valley. In 1941 the department bought most of the Mono Basin and began siphoning off the streams. Major populations of gulls, eared grebes, and red-necked phalaropes were endangered as their nesting areas diminished and became accessible to predators. In 1994 a judge ordered Los Angeles to maintain the water level in Mono Lake at 6,377 feet before diverting additional water.

Efforts to save Mono Lake (760–647–3044 for the visitor center) from being drained by the Los Angeles Department of Water and Power became one of the major environmental issues in California. Only judicial intervention required restoration of inbound streams and stabilization of the surface level of the lake. A higher lake level not only affords more protection from predators to birds nesting on the islands but also ensures that the alkalinity of the water, which has already doubled, will not increase and further affect the ecosystem.

The best place to see the tufa formations is at the South Tufa site, where rangers lead periodic hikes. You'll be amazed at the density of the nonbiting brine flies, which make up the base of the food chain here and allow for abundant bird life. Brine flies and brine shrimp attain explosive populations at Mono Lake. The Native Americans of the area, the Kuzedika, ate the flies' pupae. More than seventy species of migratory birds feed on the flies. The populations of the migrating bird species here are huge, including about 150,000 phalaropes July through August and 800,000 eared grebes August through October.

You have to get out and explore the vast Mammoth Lakes region to appreciate its historic story.

Devil's Postpile National Monument at Mammoth (established in 1911), a stunning set of basalt columns, is another treasure. Day hikes or ambitious backpacking can easily take a visitor into the wilderness, such as the John Muir Wilderness, perhaps on the John Muir or Pacific Crest Trails. In few other places will a traveler find so many accessible trails.

Mountain bikers delight in the region because of the numerous biking roads. The great winter mountain, Mammoth, noted for its ski runs, becomes a mountain-biking park in summer. You take the gondola to the top and then bike down the switchbacks, through the trees, to the bottom.

A traveler will find the requisite tourism infrastructure in the modern little mountain town of Mammoth Lakes, population 4,500.

All things considered, Mammoth has appeals that equal its more famous competitors, Yosemite and Lake Tahoe. Both those regions are better known than Mammoth, partly because they are easier to reach. Already popular as a winter ski destination, Mammoth now attracts more summer visitors.

Each aspect of the travel picture here has its own historic story. The oldest horse packing business here is Roeser's Mammoth Lakes Pack Outfit, started by the Summers family in 1915, making it also the first packer business in the eastern Sierra and one of the earliest businesses in Mammoth. Packers carried in mining supplies to the gold miners in the region long before the pleasure traveler came onto the scene.

Mammoth boasts some of the most elaborate horse packing outfits in the state. Riding on a horse can remove the huff and puff of traversing this gran-

Horse packing trips at Mammoth Lakes take visitors far into the backcountry.

ite terrain, at altitudes between 7,000 and 12,000 feet. A full-day pack trip, for example, takes you 6 miles into the wilderness to Duck Lake, revealing a backcountry that only a hiker in superb condition could experience.

The Eastern Sierra has some charming small history museums to visit en route. The Alpine County Historical Museum (530–694–2317) in Markleeville is located in a nineteenth-century schoolhouse and jail and has exhibits on area mining and ranching. The Mammoth Museum (760–934–6918) in Mammoth Lakes displays a strong collection of historic photos of the region. The Eastern California Museum (760–878–0258) in Independence has a strong Native American basketry collection.

Getting there

The most direct and delightful route in summer from San Francisco is Highway 120 east, through Yosemite and over the Yosemite High Country to Highway 395, then south. Reach Highway 120 by taking Interstate 580–205 east from the Bay Area. The all-year route, also a pleasant drive in summer, is farther north. Take Interstate 80 to Sacramento, Highway 50 to Tahoe, then Highway 89 south and east to Highway 395.

Be sure to see

Mono Lake, with its excellent visitor center, provides a full picture of the historic struggle over water. Devil's Postpile, the basaltic national monument, is a tour de force. The summer ride to the top of the Mammoth Mountain ski lift will show you a stunning display of Eastern Sierra real estate.

Best time to visit

Mammoth Lakes and the Eastern Sierras are best suited for summer touring, unless you are a winter sports enthusiast interested in skiing Mammoth Mountain.

Lodging

Mammoth Properties Reservations (3310 Main Street, Mammoth Lakes, CA 93546; 760–934–4242) is a central lodging reservation service for many condos, such as Snowcreek.

Dining

The Mogul Restaurant (1528 Tavern Road; 760–934–3039) is a family steakhouse with an ample salad bar and friendly service.

For more information

Contact Mammoth Lakes Visitors Bureau at P.O. Box 48, Mammoth Lakes, CA 93546; (888) 466–2666; www.visitmammoth.com. The contact for Devil's Postpile National Monument is c/o Sequoia and Kings Canyon National Parks, Three Rivers, CA 93271; 559–565–3341. Devils Postpile, as with each National Park and Monument entity, has its own Web site at www.nps.gov/depo.

The Sierra

The Bristlecone Pines: Oldest Living Things on Earth

Communing with the ancient bristlecone pines of the White Mountains makes the passing fashions and "everyone is famous for fifteen minutes" philosophy of our time seem fleeting indeed. Ponder your own philosophy as you wander among trees that were already ancient when Socrates posed his penetrating questions in early Greece.

The historic story

In 1957 the startling discovery was made that some bristlecone pines in the White Mountains of eastern California were much older than expected. Some gnarled specimens ring-dated to more than 4,000 years, making them the oldest living things on earth. A 9,000-year chronology of weather patterns can be established by matching the ring-dates of living trees, dead trees, and downed wood.

The tenacious bristlecones silently maintain their vigil, living in the inhospitable conditions of the White Mountains, where moisture is minimal and locked up for long periods as snow, where wind constantly prunes adventuresome branches, and where alkaline soils present as spare a nutrient base as can support plant life. Longevity of the twisted, ravaged bristlecones stands as a metaphor of adaptation to adversity.

A ranger on duty at Schulman Grove can acquaint you with two self-guided trails, the Discovery Trail and the Methuselah Trail. Take the mile-long Discovery Trail, which has plenty of photogenic trees and the Pine Alpha, the first tree that Dr. Edmund Schulman determined was more than 4,000 years old. The Methuselah Trail is longer, taking several hours, and is recommended only for the extremely fit who can hike some distance in the rarefied air.

The Ancient Bristlecone Pine Forest is a special 28,000-acre preserve within Inyo National Forest. Transport yourself to the aerie from your support base along Highway 395 at Bishop or Big Pine, convenient places for lodging and dining. Consider the outing to the bristlecones as an assault on a peak, for you will rise to almost 10,000. Make sure your car is in good condition and be sure to pace yourself, taking only very short walks. You will need to acclimatize yourself for a day or more before hiking here strenuously. Fill the tank with gasoline at Bishop, take plenty of protective clothing, and carry a gallon of water per person in your vehicle.

The view west from the bristlecone area to Owens Valley is a major panorama, aided by the clarity of the light in an environment that can be cloudless. It is interesting to imagine what the Owens Valley might have been like if its water had not been shipped off to Los Angeles.

Before you go to the bristlecones, one stop near Bishop can help tell that story. The Laws Railroad Museum (760–873–5950), on Highway 6, 4 miles northeast of Bishop, exhibits the 1883 Laws railroad depot. At that time a narrow-gauge railroad ran up and down Owens Valley, carrying passengers and agricultural abundance. Twenty-two historic buildings from the area have been transported to Laws to re-create the scene.

Originally the town was named after R. J. Laws, superintendent for the Southern Pacific Railroad. On display is Locomotive No. 9, a Slim Princess, as the narrow-gauge engines were affectionately called. A string of cars from 1960 when the railroad ceased operation, is also part of the setting.

Getting there

The bristlecone pines can be seen east from Highway 395 in the White Mountains. From Big Pine make the 23-mile drive to the bristlecones by starting east on Highway 168, also known as Westguard Pass Road. After 2 miles, stay left at the junction with Eureka Valley. Eleven miles later, a sign will direct you to the bristlecones. You pass through a forest of pinon pine and Utah juniper until you reach the nearly pure forest of bristlecones, starting at 9,500 feet. Within the Bristlecone Pine Forest, visit the Schulman Grove, at the south edge. The Patriarch Grove, lies at the north end of the forest, but the drive into this moonscapelike environment takes more than an hour on a dirt road.

Be sure to see

The ranger on duty at the bristlecones can alert you to the self-guided trails among these ancient trees.

Some of the bristlecone pines in the White Mountains are
more than 4,000 years old.

Best time to visit

You can view the bristlecones from May to October. Snow can obstruct the roads in the shoulder season and will entirely close down the area in winter.

Lodging

The Creekside Inn (725 North Main Street, Bishop, CA 93514; 760–872–3044) has a heated pool and a hot tub for hikers to relax in after an outing in the White Mountains.

Dining

Whiskey Creek (524 North Main Street; 760–873–7174) specialize in soups and steaks/prime rib for dinner. The restaurant is also open for hearty breakfasts and lunches on its outdoor deck in sunny weather.

For more information

For the bristlecones write for a brochure to Bishop Area Chamber of Commerce and Visitor Bureau, 690 North Main Street, Bishop, CA 93514; (888) 395–3952; www.bishopvisitor.com.

Stop at the visitor center while en route to the bristlecones for further information. If you approach the region from the south, stop at the Interagency Visitor Center at Lone Pine. The forest area is managed by the Forest Supervisor's Office, 873 North Main Street, Bishop, CA 93514; (760) 873–2400.

45

The Sierra

A Tall Tale of Mammoth Trees: The Giant Inland Sequoias of Sequoia and Kings Canyon National Parks

Although the California imagination sometimes suffers from inflation, certain facts of nature are indisputable: Here you can view the tallest, the most massive, and the oldest living things on earth. The decision to preserve these arboreal phenomena was a grand environmental gesture. Californians have every right to be proud.

The historic story

The tallest living earthly entities are the coast redwoods (*Sequoia sempervirens*) found along the coast north from San Francisco. Three of the tallest specimens, measuring 367 feet high, flourish in Redwood National Park near Orick in the northwest corner of the state. Chapter 28 covers them in detail.

The oldest living things on this planet are the bristlecone pines (*Pinus longaeva*) that survive in the White Mountains, a range east of Bishop. Bristlecone pines exist in other mountain settings in the Southwest, but the California trees rank as the oldest—around 4,500 years based on ring-dated core samples. Chapter 44 covers these trees.

Most massive of living things are the coast redwoods' inland cousin *Sequoiadendron giganteum*, located in pockets (fifty-three groves in all) along the western foothills of the Sierra at midstate. The giant among these is the General Sherman Tree in Sequoia National Park, east of Fresno. In 1890 the first parcel of land of this tree wonderland was set aside as a national park for future generations to enjoy. In April 2000 President Bill Clinton decreed an additional 328,000 acres of the surrounding forest land, which contains more "big trees," as a National Monument, which will be administered by the USDA Forest Service.

In deference to Civil War generals, who appeared as the most substantial figures at the time, their names were handed out to some of the giant inland sequoias, including the General Sherman and General Grant trees. You can see these marvelous and massive objects in Sequoia and Kings Canyon National Parks, twin parks comprising 1,300 square miles in the Sierra Nevada east of Fresno.

Unlike the taller coast redwood trees, which require a hike in, the inland sequoias are drive-in wonders. The largest tree, General Sherman, stands only a short walk from your car. Standing before the General Sherman Tree is akin to swimming next to a dozen blue whales in the ocean. Compared with the tree, the size of a mere human is sobering. Many of the inland sequoia trees are fully 30 feet in diameter and rise over 200 feet high.

As you proceed through the parks, it is possible to prepare yourself for the climactic encounter with General Sherman. First, pay your respect to the third largest, the General Grant Tree (267 feet high, 107.6 feet in circumference). General Grant gets the nod from many observers as the most classic illustration of this tree species because it stands alone in magnificent grandeur, beautifully proportioned. Then proceed to the second most massive tree in the Grant Grove, the General Lee. Finally, in an area of Sequoia National Park called the Giant Forest, you meet 2,100-year-old General Sherman (275 feet high, 103 feet in circumference, and 36.5 feet maximum diameter). The volume of its trunk is estimated to be 52,500 cubic feet.

The propensity to want to turn those cubic feet into board feet of salable lumber proved to be an understandable, if shortsighted, temptation of lumber interests. At the Grant Grove Visitor Center you can learn how close these priceless natural gems came to feeding a lumber mill before creation of the park. In fact, a 300-foot sequoia was cut so that a cross section could be taken to Philadelphia for the National Centennial in 1876. Most observers dismissed the purported cross section as a California hoax, a "tall tale," which was an important literary genre of the day. Trees just didn't grow this large, most people agreed. It is comforting to know that the remaining giant sequoias will now survive for at least as long as there are people to appreciate them.

Getting there

The most direct route to the most massive trees on earth is east from San

The General Grant Tree in Sequoia and Kings Canyon National Parks
bears the massive profile of an inland sequoia.

Francisco on Interstate 580, then south on Interstate 5, then east at Fresno on Highway 180 to Kings Canyon and Sequoia National Parks.

Be sure to see

To get the full benefit of the trees, scenic terrain, and many potential hikes, spend a day wandering the "Generals" Highway, entering on Highway 180 from Fresno, snaking through the park, then turning down Highway 198 to Visalia. Your vistas will include the sharp-toothed granite peaks of the Sierra, especially the view from Moro Rock. For a good hike, try the 2-mile Congress Trail in the General Sherman locale.

Best time to visit

Summer is the best time of the year to visit Sequoia and Kings Canyon.

Lodging

In Sequoia National Park stay at the new Wuksachi Village and Lodge (P.O. Box 89, Sequoia National Park, CA 93262; 888–252–5757; www. visitsequoia.com). There is also lodging available in Kings Canyon National Park.

Dining

The dining room at Wuksachi is your best dining choice.

For more information

Write ahead for a brochure to Superintendent, Sequoia/Kings Canyon National Parks, 47050 Generals Highway, Three Rivers, CA 93271; (559) 565–3341; www.nps.gov/seki.

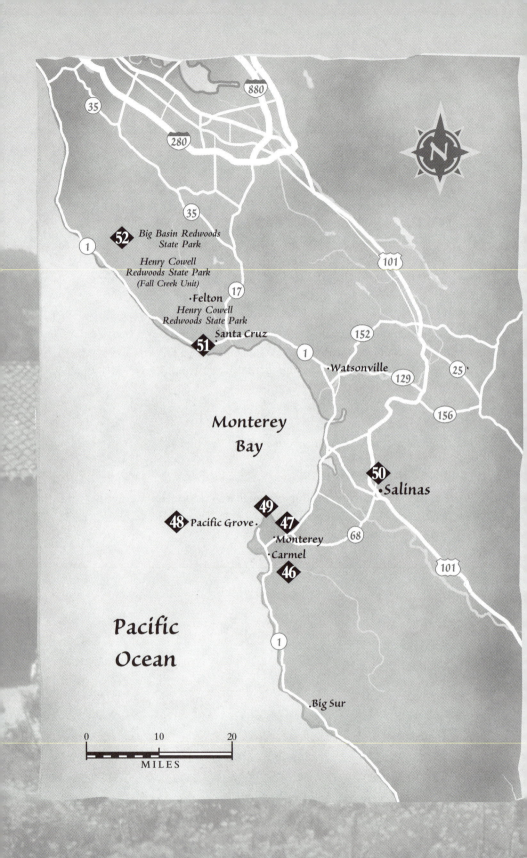

52 Big Basin Redwoods
State Park

Henry Cowell
Redwoods State Park
(Fall Creek Unit)

·Felton
Henry Cowell
Redwoods State Park

51 ·Santa Cruz

Monterey
Bay

·Watsonville

50 ·Salinas

49
48 ·Pacific Grove ·
47 ·Monterey
·Carmel
46

Pacific
Ocean

·Big Sur

N

35
880
280
35
35
1
17
1
152
129
25
156
101
68
101

0   10   20

MILES

Monterey–Big Sur and Santa Cruz

46

Monterey–Big Sur and Santa Cruz

Junipero Serra's Missions: Starting from Carmel

Few California sites contributed as much to the story of early California as did Monterey, beginning with the saga of Father Junipero Serra. Immerse yourself in the founding—secular as well as sacred—of the Golden State.

The historic story

The historic saga of Monterey extends beyond its origins. The Victorian houses of Pacific Grove grew out of a Methodist seaside camping retreat. John Steinbeck immortalized a chapter of recent Monterey history with his novel *Cannery Row*, depicting the sardine fishery and its workers.

Monterey history includes all these fascinating episodes, which remain vital today, beginning with Serra's Mission in Carmel.

Junipero Serra founded the Mission San Carlos Borromeo del Carmelo in 1770. He originally chose a site along Monterey Bay near the presidio of soldiers, but the presence of the troops and the lack of good farmland persuaded him to look farther. He found a more fertile and congenial site 5 miles south along what is now called Rio Road in Carmel. This was the second of the twenty-one missions that Franciscans founded in California between 1769 and 1821 and became the headquarters of the mission movement. The mission's potential was never realized, however, because the Indian population was too meager. Serra died here in 1784 on a simple bed consisting of three boards covered with a blanket.

Spain's King Carlos III had decided in 1768 to send missionaries to California in a bid to thwart Russian ambitions in this remote territory.

Junipero Serra, a Mallorcan Franciscan, was sent with two of his students, Francisco Palou and Juan Crespi.

Here you can pass the sarcophagus of Serra, the indefatigable mission builder and capable executive who changed the course of California life more radically than anyone else.

As a linguist and place namer, Serra decided on many of the appellations that now describe the landscape, from Carmel to San Diego. As an agriculturalist, he inaugurated the vegetable, fruit, and cattle industries for which California is now famous.

Serra has been nominated for sainthood in the Catholic Church, but the process is now stalled, largely because of the virtual enslavement and brutal treatment of the Indians in the Spanish Mission system. The Carmel Mission is a National Historic Landmark and was raised to the rank of minor basilica by the Vatican in 1960. Pope John Paul II visited the mission in 1987.

The view of the restored mission facade and front gardens suggests the fountains and vegetation that surrounded the Franciscan enclaves. The Carmel Mission has a Moorish tower and a star-shaped window.

A small museum adjacent to the church contains some remarkable artifacts, including 603 volumes in a library that Serra accumulated here. His colleague, Fermin Lasuen, cataloged the library about the year 1800, marking the books so that it is known that these were volumes used in that early era.

Aside from the library, peruse the liturgical vestments and chalices, the kitchen, and the early California oxcart. Anyone who has read about the exploits of Gaspar Portola and his heroic early exploration in California will be intrigued by an authentic leather shield and lance from one of Portola's soldiers.

Photos lining the wall of the mission museum show its appearance from the 1850s onward, including a dramatic photo of giant squash plants growing in the fertile soil adjacent to the structure. The mission deteriorated quickly when all the missions were secularized in the 1830s. However, in 1882, due to the diligent efforts of Father Casanova, the graves of Serra and Lasuen were discovered in the church. From that point on, public interest in restoring the mission has remained high.

As you leave the museum, you pass into a large courtyard that was typical of the mission style. The courtyard consists of a large fountain and elaborate gardens, all part of an active contemporary parish and school.

Beyond Carmel, the missions of Northern California could be an interesting rationale for many historic trips. Northern California missions at San Miguel, Soledad, San Juan Bautista, Santa Cruz, Santa Clara, San Francisco,

Mission founder Junipero Serra is buried at the Carmel Mission.

and Sonoma all invite the visitor—whether the original structure is now a mere adobe ruin (Soledad) or a restored, contemporary place of worship (San Francisco).

Getting there

The mission is on the south side of Carmel, adjacent to the river at 3080 Rio Road; (831) 624–3600.

Be sure to see

The mission itself is a sufficient destination. Allow time to peruse its many details, such as Serra's library.

Best time to visit

Any time of the year is good.

Lodging

Close to the mission lies an historic bed-and-breakfast, Mission Ranch Inn (26270 Dolores Street, Carmel, CA 93923; 831–624–6436), owned by

Carmel movie celebrity Clint Eastwood. You can take a room in the old Martin family ranch house from the 1870s or choose a more recent rustic cabin.

Dining

Simpson's in Carmel (San Carlos Street and Fifth Avenue; 831–624–5755) is a family-run operation offering good value.

For more information

Contact the Monterey County Convention and Visitors Bureau, P.O. Box 1770, Monterey, CA 93942-1770; (831) 649–1770; www.monterey.com.

47

Monterey–Big Sur and Santa Cruz

Monterey's Path of History: The First California Capital

From the earliest days of Spanish presence until the Gold Rush, Monterey was the principal town in California. Catch a glimpse of a time of presidio and mission—a time when the populace eagerly awaited the arrival of Boston merchant ships ready to trade an assortment of goods for California hides.

The historic story

Today you can glimpse that early world by getting a *Path of History* walking map. The map amounts to a 2.7-mile self-guided tour showing the adobes.

Monterey State Historic Park has an exceptional claim to make. It alone served as capital of California during the Spanish, Mexican, and American eras. The U.S. flag was officially raised here on July 7, 1846, effectively bringing California into the Union. The state historic park includes ten buildings that preserve the rich history of early California.

Get the map on the Custom House Plaza at the information center (831–649–7118) inside the Stanton Center. Guided tours of the historic area also leave from here.

Make your first stop at Pacific House, the first of six buildings open to the public as part of the California State Historic Park. Pacific House exhibits describe the early Spanish days.

Adjacent is the Custom House, which shows an assortment of the goods, such as metal plows and ceramics from China, that were so eagerly sought by the Californios, as the early Spanish in California were called. All goods coming in to California were supposed to go through the Custom House, built in 1827.

Plazas around Pacific House and the Custom House re-create the open architectural feel of early Monterey. Within this area with its fountain are some intriguing details from later Monterey life, such as the Italian bocce ball courts, where you won't hear a word of English. Also be sure to see California's first theater, from 1846 to 1847.

A few blocks inland are several residences that are part of the historic park. All are clearly marked on the walking map.

Writer Robert Louis Stevenson lived in the French Hotel, now called the Stevenson House, briefly in 1879.

The Casa Soberanes is an example of an early family adobe, and the Cooper-Molera family adobe contains memorabilia of these illustrious pioneers.

Consul Thomas Larkin's early house and gardens are open to the public on certain days of the week and serve as an elaborate historical museum to the early American period.

Colton Hall, the site of the first California constitutional convention, re-creates the deliberations of the late 1840s, before the capital moved to Sacramento and close to the Gold Rush riches.

All these structures are open to the public, but check at the Stanton Center for tour times. Interiors of some houses are open only during specified hours, when a guide will tell you the story. Coordinate your walk accordingly.

Richard Henry Dana's comments about California from his book *Two Years Before the Mast* can be seen sprinkled through these buildings on placards. The book, a recommended period reading, is sold at Pacific House.

Mornings are the best time to visit these structures because the early-morning light falls amply on their facades, which become shaded and darkened by later afternoon. Most early California structures, whether houses or missions, were positioned to catch the early morning light for the practical need to warm the buildings.

The gardens at these residences and adjacent to Colton Hall are elaborate and especially colorful in spring or summer. The Stevenson building offers a cozy back garden with benches. Cooper Molera boasts an ambitious herb garden, and Casa Soberanes presents an elaborate front flower garden.

Many other adobes can be viewed from the outside, using the *Path of History* map as a guide. One adobe, Casa Gutierrez, now houses a restaurant.

Getting there

Monterey is a two-hour drive south from San Francisco. The fast route is via Highway 101, cutting over to the coast at the marked Monterey exit. The more scenic route, Highway 1 along the coast, takes another hour or more.

*Consul Thomas Larkin's house in Monterey is filled with furniture
from the early American period.*

Be sure to see

The *Path of History* map, available at the Stanton Center, can alert you to all
the adobes, their precise locations, and times open.

Best time to visit

During the Monterey Adobe Walking Tour in April, more than twenty adobes
beyond the buildings in the historic park are open to the public. On July 4
there is a Hoisting of the American flag by Commodore Sloat. This reenact-
ment recalls the transition to the American era. In December, the Christmas
in the Adobes festivities feature various Christmas activities, such as drinking
Mexican chocolate and observing Victorian decor.

Lodging

The Hotel Pacific (300 Pacific Street, Monterey, CA 93940; 831–373–4815;
www.innsofmonterey.com) is an upscale lodging within walking distance of
the adobes.

Dining

Among restaurants in Monterey, try the abalone and Italian selections at historic Domenico's (831–372–3655) on the Monterey Fisherman's Wharf. Italians were among the first ethnic groups to develop the fisheries at Monterey. As tourism grew, some Italians also went into the restaurant trade. At Domenico's you'll dine with a view of sailboats, yachts, and sea lions.

For more information

Contact the Monterey County Convention and Visitors Bureau, P.O. Box 1770, Monterey, CA 93942-1770; (831) 649–1770; www.monterey.com.

The state historic park has a Web site at www.cal-parks.ca.gov. The Monterey State Historic Park headquarters is at 20 Custom House Plaza; (831) 649–7118.

48

Monterey–Big Sur and Santa Cruz

Monterey's Cannery Row Mystique: Steinbeck and the Monterey Bay Aquarium

Steinbeck and the sardines are gone, but Cannery Row lives on. Catch up with Monterey's fishing past and stewardship future as you stroll along the waterfront and Fisherman's Wharf, where travelers have become the catch of the day.

The historic story

John Steinbeck immortalized the sardine factory world of the Monterey waterfront in his novel *Cannery Row,* which appeared in 1944, just as the sardine population peaked and then mysteriously crashed. Eventually shops and restaurants took over the aging buildings. The more modern story here is the Monterey Bay Aquarium, which portrays California's growing concern for stewardship of the ocean beginning in the 1970s.

At historic Fisherman's Wharf, adjacent to Cannery Row, the sardine boats came in with their catches to fuel the canneries. Steinbeck had the genius to identify in the lives of individual Cannery Row characters the universal human condition.

When you walk along Cannery Row, you can still peer into the lab of Doc Ricketts, Steinbeck's comrade, at 800 Cannery Row. Here Ricketts maintained a weather-beaten frame "lab" where he collected sponges, anemones, barnacles, and octopi to sell to schools teaching marine biology. La Idas Cafe, one of the Row's houses of ill repute, now houses a restaurant.

The sardine-canning industry was launched here before World War I by Frank Booth, who had a salmon-canning business on the Sacramento River and wished to expand to Monterey. Noting the large numbers of sardines in the harbor, Booth engaged Norwegian Knute Hovden to develop a cannery. When World War I cut off supplies of European canned fish, it created a demand for Monterey sardines.

People lived their whole life on Cannery Row, working by day and playing hard in the bars at night. John Steinbeck, who lived here in the 1920s and early 1930s, characterized Cannery Row as "a poem, a stink, a grating noise, a quality of light, a stone, a habit, a nostalgia, a dream."

In its heyday, the Row had eighteen canneries. In 1945, just after the novel was published, production peaked at nearly a quarter-million tons of sardines. However, the silver sardines disappeared in the late 1940s, probably due to overfishing, changes in ocean current, and environmental factors.

The history of fishing in Monterey, from the early Italian families to the more recently arrived Vietnamese, is a colorful tale. Phil Anastasia, from the three-generation Italian fishing family that now operates Mike's restaurant on the wharf, recalls how his father worked as a fish peddler in the 1920s.

"He would leave the wharf at 5:00 A.M. in his Model-T and head inland to Watsonville and Castroville," says Anastasia. "Much agricultural work was then done by Japanese and Filipinos, good fish-eaters. Sometimes he drove as far as King City, staying overnight in his truck. Then he would drive back, go out in his boat, and bring in another catch. His first motorized boat, bought in 1923, cost all of $200. He was an independent fellow who spoke little English and refused to let me enroll him in Social Security when he grew old."

Monterey remains a viable fishing area, boasting the largest squid harvest in the United States.

At one end of the row, The Monterey Bay Aquarium (886 Cannery Row; 831–648–4888) is a brilliant salute to the local ocean world of California. The aquarium occupies the former Hovden Cannery, largest of the now-defunct canneries once located here. A stroke of architectural genius led the aquarium directors to incorporate elements of the existing building in the design rather than create something foreign to the site.

The aquarium is easily the main modern attraction on Cannery Row. So much has been written in recent years about this magnificent aquarium that many readers will be familiar with it. Since it opened in October 1984, millions have visited the aquarium, one of the largest in the world with more than one hundred major exhibits.

This brilliant gift of the David Packard family celebrates the offshore aquatic world of California in superb displays that include a three-story kelp forest with fishes, a live sea otter exhibit, and several hands-on exhibits, such

Novelist John Steinbeck's bust stares out from Monterey's Cannery Row.

as the Bat Ray Petting Pool. An Outer Bay wing and Splash Zone are the newer exhibits.

As you walk through the aquarium, you'll see exhibits ranging from a full-size whale model to a simulated tidal surge habitat filled with versatile creatures able to survive in an environment of pounding waves. You'll encounter remarkable creatures, such as the señorita fish, which are all female in a school—except for one female that becomes a male for procreation purposes.

The wonder of nature is so adeptly presented here that there is no need to train porpoises to jump through hoops. The concept of the aquarium wisely began its focus on the abundant California coastal fauna and flora, then spread outward to the world oceans. This approach contrasts with the concept of some aquariums to become fish warehouses of isolated exotic species from all over the planet.

Getting there

Monterey is two hours south of San Francisco via Highway 101, the fastest route. Take the marked Monterey turnoff. If you have more time, drive the Highway 1 coastal route, which is more scenic.

Be sure to see

Absorb the atmosphere of Cannery Row by walking it, noting especially the bust of Steinbeck and Doc Ricketts's lab. Be sure to stop in at the aquarium, a world-class presentation of ocean life.

Best time to visit

Any time of year is good for Cannery Row and the aquarium.

Lodging

The Monterey Plaza Hotel (400 Cannery Row, Monterey, CA 93940; 831–646–1700; www.woodsidehotels.com) locates you along Cannery Row, directly over the water. You'll see sea otters feeding in the kelp beds beneath you.

Dining

An historic wharf restaurant with local seafood is Mike's (831–372–6153), run by the several-generation fishing family of Phil Anastasia. Try the grilled salmon.

For more information

Contact the Monterey County Convention and Visitors Bureau, P.O. Box 1770, Monterey, CA 93942-1770; (831) 649–1770; www.monterey.com.

49

Monterey–Big Sur and Santa Cruz

The Enlightened, the Swells, and the Quaint: Pacific Grove, the 17-Mile Drive, and Carmel

From Monarchs to Methodists, from Pacific Grove to Pebble Beach, view stately Victorians and natural wonders, then peruse quaint Carmel.

The historic story

Beyond Serra, the Path of History adobes, and Steinbeck's Cannery Row, the Monterey Peninsula boasts several additional historic elements.

Pacific Grove, a town at the northwestern tip of the Monterey Peninsula, began as a Methodist camp in 1875. The celebrated natural phenomenon here is the gathering each October of monarch butterflies, which journey sometimes thousands of miles to overwinter in the eucalyptus and pine trees of Pacific Grove. The town celebrates with a Butterfly Parade in October.

This former Methodist seaside camp is the home of Point Pinos Lighthouse, a red-roofed structure whose Fresnel lens still warns ships along the Monterey coastal tip. Pinos has been showing the light since 1855, substantiating its claim as the oldest continuously operating lighthouse along the California coast. The lighthouse can be viewed at any time, from some distance, as you drive the Pacific Grove coast road. On Saturday and Sunday afternoons you can enter the structure.

The Victorian architecture of Pacific Grove is a carefully nurtured city amenity. Several Victorians have been turned into bed-and-breakfast inns and can be viewed along Oceanview Boulevard or a couple of blocks in from the sea. Be sure to see the Martine Inn (255 Oceanview Boulevard), Green

Pebble Beach's Lone Cypress tree, braving the assault of the wind, stands as a symbol of perseverance.

Gables Inn (104 Fifth Street), Seven Gables Inn (555 Oceanview Boulevard), Gosby House (643 Lighthouse Avenue), and Centrella B&B (612 Central Avenue).

"Our community takes much pride in preserving and celebrating its early heritage of Victorians," says Marion Martine. "The bed-and-breakfasts and our spring Victorian House Tour (in April) open them up to the public."

At the Ketchum Barn, a base for local heritage activity, or at the Pacific Grove Chamber of Commerce you can procure a walking map of the Victorians. Houses of historical note have placards on them indicating their date of construction and first owner. A walking tour of the Victorians amounts to a pleasant afternoon in Pacific Grove.

After enjoying Pacific Grove, take a ride on the 17-Mile Drive past the Pebble Beach Golf Course and the homes of the wealthy.

The 17-Mile Drive through the Del Monte Forest presents an appealing view of trees, coastline, and lavish private homes. Trees include prime stands of Monterey pine and cypress. The coastline affords ample places to walk or picnic, such as Spanish Bay, and good sites for observing sea life, especially at Seal Rock and Bird Rock.

The Lone Cypress stop salutes a singular tree whose gnarled appearance—growing out of the rocks and struggling constantly in the face of winds—stands as a symbol of tenacity and perseverance. Hundreds of sumptuous homes lend a fairy-tale aura to the woodsy 17-Mile Drive ambience.

Carmel is an appealing small village to stroll if you like to browse art galleries and shops. Look for the *Gallery Tour* brochure in the shops here. Ask for directions to poet Robinson Jeffers's Tor House (26304 Ocean View Avenue). Jeffers made his reputation celebrating the natural environment but without seeing man as an improvement on the scene. Carmel goes to great lengths to maintain its high-tone village exclusivity through zoning rules designed to keep out the hoi polloi. At the south end of Carmel you'll find one of the loveliest beaches in California, little-used Carmel River Beach, which includes a parking lot, ample sand, and crashing surf—excellent ingredients for a beach walk. The setting is enhanced by the view of Point Lobos offshore.

Getting there

The Monterey Peninsula is a two hour drive from San Francisco via Highway 101. Take the marked Monterey exit. If you have more time, take the scenic coast route, Highway 1.

Be sure to see

This is a driving and walking excursion. Drive the coastal road through Pacific Grove, perhaps getting out for a fresh-air walk among the Victorians. Then motor the 17-Mile Drive with some choice stops, perhaps at the Lone Cypress. Finally, park in downtown Carmel and peruse the quaint shops, poet Jeffers's house, and the town's lovely beach.

Best time to visit

Any time of the year is good for this trip. In April Pacific Grove hosts a Victorian Home Tour and Good Old Days. On these days several of the Victorians of Pacific Grove beyond the bed-and-breakfast inns are open to the public.

Lodging

The Gosby House Inn (643 Lighthouse Avenue, Pacific Grove, CA 93950; 800–527–8828; www.foursisters.com) is one choice among the historic Victorian lodgings in Pacific Grove.

Dining

Fandango (223 Seventeenth Street; 831–372–3456) offers an eclectic Continental menu emphasizing Mediterranean food and a mesquite grill. Try the rack of lamb or paella.

For more information

Contact the Monterey County Convention and Visitors Bureau, P.O. Box 1770, Monterey, CA 93942-1770; (831) 649–1770; www.monterey.com.

For information on Pacific Grove's historic walks, call (800) 656–6650.

50

Monterey–Big Sur and Santa Cruz

John Steinbeck's Salinas: The Okies of *The Grapes of Wrath*

> The Salinas Valley is the place to witness the amazing historic story of California agriculture, which feeds the nation with its abundance. But the story also has a darker side—as evoked by Salinas native John Steinbeck in his novel *The Grapes of Wrath*.

The historic story

Seventeen miles inland from Monterey lies Salinas, birthplace of celebrated author John Steinbeck (1902–1968) and site of the National Steinbeck Center, which opened in 1998. The center honors the author with displays celebrating his classic novels and serves as a cultural venue for the region.

The Dust Bowl Depression-era migration of Okies to California was one of the uglier stories of opportunity in the Golden State. California stationed police officers at the state line to turn back the migrants. People were turned back at Needles, where Highway 66 crossed into California, rejected on the basis of appearance and presumed financial status. This was one of the few cases in U.S. history where American citizens could not freely travel within their own country. The U.S. Supreme Court struck down the state's law in the case of *Edwards vs. California*.

Everyone agrees that the Okies had it tough. Just how tough is hard to imagine, but John Steinbeck's *The Grapes of Wrath* provides a glimpse. Okies were escaping the Dust Bowl, approximately 150,000 square miles that include the Oklahoma and Texas panhandles and adjacent parts of Colorado, New Mexico, and Kansas. The area has light soil, low rainfall, and high winds. After early use of the land for grazing, farmers plowed up the soil to plant winter wheat. A drought between 1934 and 1937 and high winds kicked up

John Steinbeck's family house can be seen at 132 Central Avenue in Salinas.

huge dust storms over the denuded and vulnerable land, exposed without its grass anchor. The dust storms suffocated people and buried buildings. More than half the population moved out, mainly west to California. These migrants were called Okies.

Steinbeck was the great chronicler of the Okies. His main characters are the Joads, a family that loses its farm through foreclosure and leaves the Oklahoma Dust Bowl for California in order to find work. The eldest generation has the solace of religion, the middle generation has a dogged determination, but the youngest has little to hope for. A reader gets a feel for decent people at the utter end of their resources. Angered by the brutal exploitation of migrant workers, Tom Joad becomes a labor organizer.

The novel was published in 1939, won the Pulitzer prize in 1940, and became a popular movie directed by John Ford and starring Henry Fonda. *The Grapes of Wrath* was labeled "vulgar" by the Kern County Board of Supervisors and banned there from 1939 to 1941. Steinbeck was denounced by the Associated Farmers and supported by Eleanor Roosevelt. His vivid depiction of the lot of migrant workers outraged capitalists and heartened radicals, though Steinbeck was not an ideologue. He learned from practical observation, traveling the San Joaquin Valley in 1938 with photographer Harry Bristol. Steinbeck won the Nobel Prize in 1962.

It took Salinas a long time to come to terms with native—though not favorite—son Steinbeck. Salinas saw itself, warts and all, in Steinbeck's works, which caused the city fathers to ban his books. There were even burnings of Steinbeck's literary efforts, and the book was banned in Bakersfield. Today some members of the community still resent Steinbeck's portrayal of Salinas, even as they realize that Steinbeck-related tourism is more than a cottage industry here. His sympathetic focus on the poor, the eccentric, and the dispossessed angered those at the apex of the power structure.

Getting there

Salinas is 105 miles south of San Francisco on Highway 101. Take the Main Street exit to reach the Steinbeck Center.

Be sure to see

In Salinas visit Steinbeck's birthplace at 132 Central Avenue. The restored Victorian now houses a restaurant with open-seating lunch 11:30 A.M. to 2:00 P.M. Steinbeck's upstairs room, the front garret, is closed to the public because the stairs are too steep for these litigious times. However, at first-floor level you can wander from room to room, all used in the luncheon operation, and see photos on the wall, including a cherubic picture of Steinbeck at age four. A gift shop in the basement, the Best Cellar, stocks copies of his works.

The main cultural attraction to visit is the National Steinbeck Center at One Main Street. Interactive exhibits re-create the author's life and works. At the *Cannery Row* exhibit you will smell the fish and hear the seagulls. The *East of Eden* display includes the cool air of a lettuce boxcar. One special gem at the Center is "Rocinante," the custom camper that Steinbeck drove across America while writing *Travels with Charlie*.

A possible minor stop to consider is the Steinbeck Library at 350 Lincoln, which exhibits a sculpture of the author and some photo blow-ups on the walls.

The passionate Steinbeck appreciator may want to make a final stop, a look at Steinbeck's grave in the substantial Hamilton Family burial site at the Garden of Memories cemetery. The Hamiltons were his mother's side of the family.

Best time to visit

The National Steinbeck Center sponsors a multifaceted Steinbeck Festival each August, featuring speakers, tours, movies of his works, and theater.

Lodging

For lodging, Monterey/Carmel is only a short drive away. Try one of the classic small inns of Carmel, such as the Dolphin Inn (P.O. Box 1900, Fourth and San Carlos, Carmel, CA 93921; 831–624–5356).

Dining

A meal at the Steinbeck House would be appropriate. Be sure to call ahead to make a reservation.

For more information

Steinbeck's Salinas venues include his birthplace, the Steinbeck House (132 Central Avenue), which serves luncheons on weekdays; call (831) 424–2735.

The National Steinbeck Center is at One Main Street, Salinas, CA 93901; (831) 775–4720; www.steinbeck.org. The Steinbeck Library is at 350 Lincoln Avenue; (831) 758–7311.

The local tourism source is the Salinas Valley Area Chamber of Commerce, 119 East Alisal Street, Salinas, CA 93902; (831) 424–7611; www.salinaschamber.com.

51

Monterey–Big Sur and Santa Cruz

Santa Cruz's Story:
The Beach Boardwalk and
Progressive University

Gentle climate and seaside location have made Santa Cruz a popular tourist destination since 1865. Stroll the historic boardwalk and resurgent downtown. Tour the town's Victorian heritage—then take a white-knuckle ride on a classic wooden coaster.

The historic story

Santa Cruz first existed as a Franciscan mission, Mission La Exaltacion de la Santa Cruz. Today you can locate the old mission site from many vantage points in Santa Cruz by looking for the dominant white spire of the Holy Cross Church, on the same hilltop.

When Fermin Lasuen established the Santa Cruz Mission, (twelfth of twenty-one in the chain), the work of conversion and church-building moved quickly at first. Grazing grass, berries, redwood and pine lumber, and water were plentiful. But by 1832 the mission had vanished, a victim of secularization, earthquake, and neglect. Today you can see a two-third-scale replica of the structure, built in 1931, at 126 High Street.

Fueled by the early prosperity of lumber milling, lime mining for use in cement, leather tanning, and tourism, the region prospered, creating a legacy of lovely Victorian architecture from 1880 to 1900. The architectural heritage of Santa Cruz can be observed in residential areas, where many of the original homes have been restored.

Santa Cruz's mile-long pier is the longest in California.

The downtown has changed dramatically in recent years. Until 1989 a visitor would walk down Pacific Avenue, the old main street, which had been turned into a walker's Garden Mall. The central building here was the yellow-brick Cooper House, originally the Santa Cruz Courthouse, built in 1895. Next door to Cooper House was the Octagon, built in 1882. Once the Santa Cruz Hall of Records, the Octagon now houses a museum gift shop. Most of the major brick structures on this mall walk, including Cooper House, were damaged by the 1989 quake, causing loss of life and property, and had to be bulldozed. Reconstruction in the area got off to a slow start. The heart of the community had been destroyed, but the Santa Cruz downtown is now viable again.

One structure of note is the new McPherson Center (705 Front Street; 831–429–1964), home of The Museum of Art and History. Be sure to see the interpretation of Santa Cruz history titled "Where the Redwoods Meet the Sea," which focuses on the area's complex economy—from redwood lumbering in the hills to the agricultural fecundity around Watsonville. The McPherson Center also hosts changing art exhibits and is the venue for many local cultural happenings.

Some main attractions, each with its historic elements, include the Santa Cruz Boardwalk and the University of California Santa Cruz campus.

The Santa Cruz Beach Boardwalk (831–426–7433), located at 400 Beach Street, was built in 1904, burned down in 1906, and rebuilt in 1907. Its large roller coaster, the Giant Dipper, is a classic wooden structure from 1924 that has carried millions of riders on white-knuckle trips. The boardwalk has three arcades, a wide beachfront, and the Coconut Grove Ballroom, which features big bands. The centerpiece of the boardwalk is the merry-go-round. A Danish woodcarver, Charles I. D. Looff, delivered the first seventy hand-carved horses in 1911. The carousel still operates today, along with its original 342-piece Ruth band organ, built in 1894.

West of the boardwalk, the Santa Cruz Municipal Wharf offers a pleasant stroll, fish markets, seafood restaurants, and pier fishing or deep-sea fishing excursions. If you walk out on the mile-long pier, the longest on the Pacific Coast, you'll get plenty of bracing sea air and a splendid view looking back at Santa Cruz.

The University of California Santa Cruz campus (Bay and High Streets; 831–459–0111) is tucked among 2,000 acres of redwoods and rolling grasslands on the outskirts of town. The campus is interesting to visit for its architectural innovations and natural setting. From the university hills you'll see panoramic views of Santa Cruz and Monterey Bay. Self-guided tour maps are available at a kiosk a quarter mile from the main entrance.

Pause by the side of the road as you enter to note the old Cowell Ranch building from the limestone-mining and cattle-ranching days.

One of the special aspects of Santa Cruz as an oceanside location is its excellent surfing. The surf area is also unusual because it can be viewed up close by the public. Simply walk or drive out West Cliff Drive to the Mark Abbott Memorial Lighthouse, which houses the Santa Cruz Surfing Museum (831–420–6289), with displays celebrating the decades the sport has flourished. From the cliffs at the lighthouse you'll look out at Steamer Lane, the choice surfing area.

Getting there

Santa Cruz is two hours south of San Francisco along Coast Highway 1. The 70-mile route is faster but less scenic if you take Highway 101 south and cut across the mountains on Highway 17.

Be sure to see

The historic roller coaster and carousel at the Beach Boardwalk, the phoenix-like rise of the downtown area from the 1989 quake, and the University of California campus are the main attractions.

Best time to visit

Any time of the year is good for Santa Cruz.

Lodging

For a cozy B&B, try the Babbling Brook Inn (1025 Laurel Street, Santa Cruz, CA 95060; 831–427–2437; www.babblingbrookinn.com). Each room is fashioned around the theme of an Impressionist painter.

Dining

For a candlelit dinner within the city, choose the Gabriella Cafe (910 Cedar Street; 831–457–1677), a Northern Italian restaurant where the potato-leek soup might precede a portabello mushroom entree.

For more information

Contact the Santa Cruz County Conference and Visitors Council, 1211 Ocean Street, Santa Cruz, CA 96060; (800) 833–3494; www.santacruzca.org.

52

Monterey–Big Sur and Santa Cruz

Big Basin: The Redwoods and Roaring Camp Railroad

> Get to the origin of the redwood conservation movement at California's first state park—where the impetus to save coastal redwoods began. Then ride on an authentic steam train from the lumbering era.

The historic story

Big Basin was the first state park and is, in many ways, the most significant of all California state parks. The park was created in 1902 as a result of public distaste over the impending doom of virgin redwoods in this area.

Though no one person can be credited with founding the conservation movement in California, certainly one pioneer deserves special mention—Andrew P. Hill, photographer, painter, conservationist, and propagandist.

An ugly incident at Felton in 1899 kindled Hill's rage. On assignment from a British publication, Hill went to the Felton area to photograph redwood trees because he felt the best specimens could be found there. But an irate landowner threw Hill off his land and screamed at him, "This is *MY* property. These are *MY* trees. No one can photograph them unless I say so."

As a fuming Hill waited at the depot for the train ride back to San Jose, an idea suddenly occurred to him.

"The thought flashed through my mind that these trees, because of their size and antiquity, were among the natural wonders of the world," he later wrote. "They should be saved for posterity. Thus was born my idea of saving the redwoods."

Hill was tireless in this pursuit. He organized a meeting with David Starr Jordan of Stanford and representatives of other colleges and institutions,

The Roaring Camp steam train rides into the redwood-logging region near Santa Cruz.

including the Sierra Club. Together they agreed to focus on Big Basin rather than other areas because Big Basin had not yet been logged. The group formed a committee that went to survey Big Basin. Around a campfire one night on Sempervirens Creek they passed the hat, collecting the first $32 of the millions that would eventually be needed to save sizable chunks of redwood real estate.

At Big Basin you can hike or drive to the site, called Slippery Rock, opposite Sempervirens Falls, and read the marker that recalls this historic camp:

"The first state park. A group of conservationists led by Andrew P. Hill camped at the base of Slippery Rock on May 18, 1900, and formed the Sempervirens Club to preserve the redwoods of Big Basin. Their efforts resulted in deeding 3,800 acres of primeval forests to the state of California on September 20, 1902. This marked the beginning of the California State Park System."

Near Felton you can board the Roaring Camp and Big Trees Narrow-Gauge Railroad, one of the last steam-powered trains still running. The tracks twist around a 5-mile loop through redwood groves. Back in the 1880s lumberjacks and pioneers used this train to haul out lumber and shingles. During the hour-long trip you switchback up some of the steepest grades ever built for a railroad.

At Roaring Camp you can see a covered bridge and visit a reconstructed 1880's General Store that sells items from western garb to a complete line of books for the rail buff.

At Bear Mountain you can get off the train for a picnic or a hike in the redwoods and then catch a later train back to depot headquarters. The conductor gives a competent commentary on the flora of the region during the stop and as the train moves. At a pause in a "cathedral" of redwoods, he describes how new redwood trees sprout in a circle around the deceased mother tree.

Near the boarding platform you can see the steam-powered sawmill. In the spirit of the setting, meals of chuckwagon barbecued beef are served. Local musicians sing ballads of the lumbering West and other country-and-western themes.

Another popular ride is the Moonlight Steam Train Dinner from June to October, with singing and dancing under the stars.

The railroad is rich in legend and history. Riding it today can help you approximate the time when passengers from the East Bay, boarding in Newark, could ride down the East Bay shore, cross the Santa Clara Valley, then train over the mountains to resort pleasures here in the redwoods or beach attractions at Santa Cruz. These Picnic Trains or Suntan Specials are gone forever, but the present Roaring Camp Railroad excites considerable nostalgia.

Five locomotives constitute the rail company's main holdings, ranging from the *Kahuku*, a twelve-ton Baldwin locomotive from 1890, to the *Dixiana*, a forty-two-ton Shay locomotive from 1912. The *Kahuku* was once used to pull sugarcane on Hawaiian plantations.

Getting there

Big Basin lies on ocean-facing slopes about 23 miles northwest of Santa Cruz and 9 miles northwest of Boulder Creek on Highway 236. The entrance to Roaring Camp is off Graham Hill Road in Felton, just south of the Mt. Hermon Road exit off Highway 17 in Scotts Valley. You can also enter from the nearby parking lot of Henry Cowell Redwoods State Park. If you plan to visit the train and Henry Cowell Park, go directly to the park and walk to the train. Big Basin and the train/Henry Cowell park are about thirty-five minutes apart on winding roads.

Be sure to see

Big Basin Redwoods State Park is the historic park in the Santa Cruz Mountains. Roaring Camp and Big Trees Railroad is the authentic rail experience to savor.

Best time to visit

Summertime is especially delightful here, when the cool of the redwoods contrasts with the heat of exposed areas. Roaring Camp holds a "railroad Olympics" each July; contestants compete at driving rail spikes and pumping authentic railroad handcars.

Lodging

Return to Santa Cruz for lodging. The Westcoast Santa Cruz Hotel (175 West Cliff Drive, Santa Cruz, CA 95060; 800–426–0670; www.westcoasthotels. com) is a classic lodging on the cliffs overlooking the boardwalk.

Dining

Bittersweet Bistro, in the adjacent town of Rio Del Mar (787 Rio Del Mar Boulevard; 831–662–9799), has raised the fine-dining standards of Santa Cruz. Try the grilled lamb sirloin or the linguini and clams.

For more information

Contact Big Basin Redwoods State Park at (831) 338–8860; www.cal-parks.ca.gov.

Contact Roaring Camp and Big Trees Narrow Gauge Railroad at (831) 335–4484; www.roaringcamp.com.

Big Basin and Roaring Camp are in the Santa Cruz region. For more regional information contact the Santa Cruz County Conference and Visitors Council, 1211 Ocean Street, Santa Cruz, CA 96060; (800) 833–3494; www.santacruzca.org.

Index